MARSHA WEIL, BRUCE JOYCE
and BRIDGET KLUWIN

PERSONAL
MODELS OF TEACHING

EXPANDING YOUR
TEACHING REPERTOIRE

PRENTICE-HALL, INC., ENGLEWOOD CLIFFS, NEW JERSEY 07632

Library of Congress Cataloging in Publication Data

WEIL, MARSHA.
    Personal models of teaching.
    (Expanding your teaching repertoire)

    Includes index.
    1. Teaching.   I. Joyce, Bruce R., joint author.
II. Kluwin, Bridget, joint author.   III. Title.
IV. Series.
LB1025.2.W446   371.1'02   77-6638
ISBN 0-13-657767-9
ISBN 0-13-657759-8 pbk.

371
.102
W422p

This book is dedicated to our parents

GRACE AND MITCHELL LEWIS
URSULA AND LOUIS JOYCE

Printed in the United States of America

10   9   8   7   6   5   4   3   2   1

PRENTICE-HALL INTERNATIONAL, INC., *London*
PRENTICE-HALL OF AUSTRALIA PTY. LIMITED, *Sydney*
PRENTICE-HALL OF CANADA, LTD., *Toronto*
PRENTICE-HALL OF INDIA PRIVATE LIMITED, *New Delhi*
PRENTICE-HALL OF JAPAN, INC., *Tokyo*
PRENTICE-HALL OF SOUTHEAST ASIA PTE. LTD., *Singapore*
WHITEHALL BOOKS LIMITED, *Wellington, New Zealand*

CONTENTS

FOREWORD

I have been using *Models of Teaching* over the last eight years and I think that my favorite family is the personal family. *Personal Models of Teaching*, as the name implies, deals primarily with the self, with things within us, such as feelings and emotions. These have too often been ignored in our classrooms.

One of the best things about the models in this book is that they are based on a very positive view of the abilities of both the teacher and student. In the Nondirective Teaching Model, the assumption is that the student has the ability to recognize, analyze, and work through his or her own problems with the help of the teacher. In Synectics, it is stressed that all people have creative abilities within them—ready to be tapped and used to make them more interesting, expressive human beings.

In both these models, the teacher's role is quite different from the normal role as director of the classroom and dispenser of knowledge. The teacher takes on the role of listener and focuser in the Nondirective Model. The teacher acts as the stimulator of creative abilities through the use of analogies in Synectics. As a teacher who has used both models, I can say there is little in teaching that is quite as exciting as watching children light up as they begin to describe something using analogies, or watching a young person begin to believe in his or her own ability to work through personal problems.

I have used Synectics with children as young as four years old. I have seen them use analogies to describe trees and houses in ways that radiated creative thinking. When I use the stategy with high school students, the first response usually is, "You got to be kidding; you want me to be a piece of celery?" But they do become a piece of celery, or a snowflake, and they do use metaphors to describe their schools, their parents, or themselves. Their expressions are filled with feeling and life, and it's fun.

I have used the Nondirective strategy in many situations. It is an ideal strategy to use when you do not want to control the substance of a conversation. The problem and the solution come from the student. When I worked with college students who were making career decisions, the Nondirective Model enabled me to act as a listener and a clarifier while they decided what they wanted. A third-grade child who is having trouble with other children on the playground can be helped by the Nondirective Model to examine the problem and arrive at a solution that is the child's own choice, rather than one that is imposed by the teacher. Nondirective techniques offer a teacher a way of helping children understand their problems and arrive at their own solutions, rather than having the teacher in the role of decision-maker and problem-solver.

One caution should be observed when using counseling methods such as Non-directive Teaching. Teachers are not primarily therapists, and this model should not be expected to make a teacher into one. It is an interesting model, one that helps teachers and children relate more closely over problems, but it is *teaching*, not therapy.

Personal Models of Teaching can be used in a wide range of settings. I have used them in both open classrooms and self-contained classrooms. These models deal with dimensions of the child that we normally neglect, and they do so in a way that is both productive and enjoyable.

Michael McKibbin

San Jose State University

ACKNOWLEDGMENTS

We owe an enormous debt to a large number of colleagues and students throughout the United States. At Teachers' College, Columbia University, Rhoada Wald, Michael McKibbin, Michael Feller, Christina Gullion, Kathryn O'Donnell, Clark Brown, Robert Gower, Jill Levine, Kay Vandergrift, Joseph Kelly, Gene Rude, Deane Flood, Daisy Reed, Sam Stewart, Charlie Abate, plus many teachers, school administrators, professors, and researchers helped us develop and test the early versions of what ultimately became these materials. Karl Schmidt, then of Science Research Associates, worked very closely with us and with Drs. Wald and McKibbin to build the first widely disseminated materials. David Hunt, Ed Sullivan, Joann Greenwood, Joyce Noy, Roma Reid and others at the Ontario Institute for Studies in Education helped to structure and conduct some of the most important training research we were able to do and helped us embark on the first research with children.

Roger Pankratz of Western Kentucky University, Carolyn Ellner of the Claremont Graduate School of Education, Pat Murphy of the University of Minnesota, Greta Morine-Dershimer of the Far West Laboratory, Paul and Margaret Collins of the California State University of Hayward worked individually and together with us in developing and testing teacher training ideas relevant to this Models of Teaching series. Christopher Clark, Penelope Peterson, Ronald Marx,

Jane Anton, and Janet Crist-Witzel of the Stanford Center for Research and Development in Teaching helped harden our ideas and conducted a series of investigations with us that advanced our thinking.

National Teacher Corps, especially William Smith, James B. Steffenson, and Paul Collins, helped us greatly. Their colleagues, Art Brill, Jack Ether, Dan Ganeles, Bev Elender, and Jan Hillson provided many interesting ideas and in many ways opened up new areas of research and development before we had perceived them ourselves.

Floyd Waterman of the University of Nebraska, Rupert Trujillo of the University of New Mexico, Bud Meyers of the University of Vermont, Berj Harootunian of Syracuse University, and Chet Hill and Dave Marsh of the University of Southern California also worked with us in a variety of ways. Members of the Allendale School staff in Pasadena, California, including Alma Hill and Elsa Brizzi, advanced our thinking about the adaptation of *Models of Teaching* to multicultural settings; Claudia Ulbrecht, Jennifer Bird-in-Ground, Muata, and Joel Morine contributed imaginative demonstration lessons.

The Bureau of Educational Professions Development supported some of the most difficult early work; we are especially indebted to Allen Schmeider for his counsel and advice during that period. The present materials were piloted in the Corps Member Training Institute of National Teacher Corps. Drs. Smith, Waterman, Pankratz, and McKibbin, Paul Collins, Jim Steffensen, and Beryl Nelson were powerful colleagues during that experience. The National Education Association piloted the training of teachers to operate teacher centers based on *Models of Teaching*. John Leeke of the NEA staff and Ruth Foster of the Omaha Public Schools were especially helpful to us during that experiment.

Finally, we acknowledge with gratitude the contributions of the people who developed the concepts around which the various models are based: Fannie Shaftel, Professor Emeritus of Stanford University, Richard Suchman, Bill Gordon of Synectics Incorporated, Donald Oliver of Harvard University, James P. Shaver of the University of Utah, and other colleagues are gratefully acknowledged.

Marsha Weil
Bruce Joyce

**Supplementary audio-visual materials to accompany this text
can be ordered from:**

> Dr. Bruce Joyce
> Center for Research and Development in Teaching
> Stanford University
> Stanford, California 94305

INTRODUCTION

A POINT OF VIEW ABOUT TEACHING

How do we think of ourselves as professional teachers and educators? We are responsible for many types of instruction, for helping our students grow in self-awareness and in their ability to relate to others, for clarifying values, for promoting moral development, and for a host of other objectives. Our responsibilities can conveniently be described in three categories: responsibility for the personal growth of our students, responsibility for their social development and preparation for national and world citizenship, and responsibility for their mastery of academic subjects, including the basic skills of reading and computation that are so essential to contemporary life. In order to accomplish these objectives we work in schools, and within these in classrooms, learning centers, and libraries. Much of our contact with students is formal: they are assembled in classes to take one or more courses from us. But we have much informal contact with them as well. In addition, we teachers work either relatively alone or in teaching teams, perhaps with paid and volunteer aides assisting us.

To carry out these multiple responsibilities, we are required to engage in several professional roles, often simultaneously. We are counselors, facilitators, instructional managers, curriculum designers, academic instructors, evaluators of instruction, and, reluctantly, disciplinarians. To fill these roles, we draw on a variety of models of teaching. There are presently available to us many alternatives for organizing and carrying out learning experiences, some formal and traditional and others casual and emergent.

Our initial preparation for teaching is relatively brief, considering the diverse responsibilities and the complexity of our roles. The preparation we receive prior to entering the classroom takes place in university courses and in the relatively short apprenticeship that we call "student teaching" or "internship."

When we begin our teaching, we perceive only dimly that we must master multiple roles. Gradually, as we get our bearings, we begin to see teaching as a cluster of differing roles and responsibilities. We then seek alternative ways to fulfill our tasks as teachers, and we begin to broaden our perspective on the nature of teaching. Finally, we spend the greater part of our professional lives attempting to improve our competence and to sharpen our skills. As we become more professional, we try to expand the ways we can be meaningful to our students—we master more roles.

The authors see the development of professional competence in teaching as an increased ability to play the various assigned roles more effectively. Our point of view is that a large part of this competence consists in mastering a repertoire of approaches to teaching that can be used to carry out these roles. We believe that competence is expanded in two ways: first, by increasing the *range of teaching strategies* that we are able to employ; second, by *becoming increasingly skillful* in the use of each of these strategies.

Different roles *require* different teaching strategies. In our earlier book, *Models of Teaching* (1972), we described our search for teaching strategies that are based on defendable theories about how people learn, grow, and develop. Some of these theory-based models of teaching are more appropriate to some objectives than to others. For example, some are specially tailored to help students grow in self-awareness and strength of self-concept. Others are more appropriate for improving human relations in the classroom and helping students clarify their social values. Yet others are more appropriate for the mastery of subject matter. Some models of teaching are quite narrow in their focus, and others are useful for a wide variety of purposes.

A model of teaching consists of guidelines for designing educational activities and environments. It specifies ways of teaching and learning that are intended to achieve certain kinds of goals. A model includes a rationale, a theory that justifies it and describes what it is good for and why; the rationale may be accompanied by empirical evidence that it "works." In *Models of Teaching*, we deliberately selected models representing different frames of reference toward educational goals and methods. That book was written for the purpose of helping teachers explore a variety of philosophical and psychological positions, which they could then make come to life in the classroom.

We discovered models of teaching in many sources. Educators, psychologists, sociologists, systems analysts, psychiatrists, and many others have all developed theoretical positions about learning and teaching. Curriculum development projects, schools and school districts, and organizations representing particular curriculum areas or disciplines have also developed a large number of approaches to teaching and learning. The task of selection began with compiling a very long list of sources of models. Included were the works of counselors and therapists such as Erikson

(1950), Maslow (1962), and Rogers (1951), as well as those of learning theorists such as Ausubel (1963), Bruner (1966), and Skinner (1957); developmental psychologists such as Hunt (1971), Kohlberg (1966), and Piaget (1952); and philosophers such as Broudy (1965), Dewey (1916), and James (1899). Curriculum development in the academic subjects provided many examples, as did group dynamics. Patterns of teaching from great experimental schools such as Summerhill made their way onto our list. Altogether, more than eighty theorists, schools, and projects were identified, far more than any teacher would be able to master during a career.

Gradually, we began to group the models on the basis of their chief emphases—the ways they approached educational goals and means. We eventually organized them into four families:

1. Social Interaction Models. These emphasize the relationships of the individual to society or to other persons. They focus on the processes by which reality is socially negotiated. Consequently, with respect to goals, models from this orientation give priority to the improvement of the individual's ability to relate to others, the improvement of democratic processes, and the improvement of the society. It must be stressed that the social-relations orientation does not assume that these goals constitute the *only* important dimension of life. While social relations may be emphasized more than other domains, social theorists are also concerned with the development of the mind and the self, and the learning of academic subjects. (It is the rare theorist in education who is not concerned with more than one aspect of the learner's development, or who does not use more than one aspect of the environment to influence the learner's development.)

2. Information Processing Models. The second large family of models share an orientation toward the information processing capability of students and toward the systems that can improve their information processing capability. Information processing refers to the ways people handle stimuli from the environment, organize data, sense problems, generate concepts and solutions to problems, and employ verbal and nonverbal symbols. Some information processing models are concerned with the ability of the learner to solve problems, and thus emphasize productive thinking; others are concerned with general intellectual ability. Some emphasize the teaching of strategies derived from the academic disciplines. Again, however, it must be stressed that nearly all models from this family are also concerned with social relationships and the development of an integrated, functioning self.

3. Personal Models. The third family share an orientation toward the individual and the development of selfhood. They emphasize the processes by which individuals construct and organize their unique reality. Frequently, they focus on the emotional life of the individual. It is expected that the focus on helping individuals to develop a productive relationship with their environment and to view themselves as capable persons will produce richer interpersonal relations and a more effective information processing capability.

4. Behavior Modification Models. This fourth type of model has evolved from attempts to develop efficient systems for sequencing learning tasks and shaping behavior by manipulating reinforcement. Exponents of reinforcement theory, such as Skinner (1957), have developed these models and operant conditioning as their central mechanism. They are frequently referred to as behavior modification theories because they emphasize changing the external behavior of the learners and describe them in terms of visible behavior rather than underlying and unobservable behavior. Operant conditioning has been applied to a wide variety of goals, in education and other areas, ranging from military training to the improvement of interpersonal behavior and even to therapy. It is represented by a large number of models, some of which are media-oriented (such as programmed stategies) and some of which are oriented to interactive teaching (such as the use of tokens to shape social behavior).

These families of models are by no means antithetical or mutually exclusive. The actual prescriptions for developing the instructional activities and learning environments that emerge from some of them—even those classified in different families—are remarkably similar. Also, within the families, models share many features with respect both to goals and to the kinds of means they recommend. All educational activities evoke different meanings in different people. In this sense, everything we do is personal. Similarly, most of our experiences, especially educational ones, involve some intellectual or information processing activity.

Over the years, we have discussed our original classifications with many of our colleagues, agreeing with many of their objections and rethinking our position. In this text, we have reclassified a few of the models. In general, we feel it is the basic framework of families that has become a powerful intellectual tool for teachers and curriculum planners, rather than the specific classification of individual models. However, we have made an effort to classify models according to the most prominent goal or features that distinguish them from another family.

In this three-volume series, we are concerned only with models from the information processing, social, and personal families. It seemed to us that there are presently available several excellent sources on the adaptation of behavior modification and its variations to the classroom. We therefore decided to concentrate on models that are less available in the literature. Models from these three families are listed in Figures 1A-1C.

To us, growth in teaching is the increasing mastery of a variety of models of teaching and the ability to use them effectively. Some philosophies of teacher education maintain that a teacher should master a single model and utilize it well. We believe that very few teachers are so limited in capacity. Most of us can quite easily develop a repertoire of six or eight models of teaching, which we can use in order to carry out our roles. We should choose our "basic" repertoire to meet the needs generated by our teaching assignment. Certain models are more appropriate for some curriculums than for others; that is, the curriculum helps define our role and the kinds of competencies that we need. For example, a secondary school science teacher of biology who is using Biological Sciences Study Committee materials will want to master the particular kind of inductive approach that fits best with those materials; an elementary school social studies teacher who is helping children study values may want to master one of the models appropriate to clarifying values and analyzing public issues. Once a teacher master the "basic" repertoire of models, he or she can then expand it by learning new models and by combining and transforming the basic ones to create new ones. In the midst of a social studies unit, a teacher may use a highly specific model to help children master map skills, and combine this model with group-dynamic models that help students attack social issues. A highly skilled performance in teaching blends the variety of models appropriately and embellishes them. Master teachers create new models of teaching and test them in the course of their work.

Model	Major Theorist	Mission or Goals for Which Most Applicable
Inductive Thinking Model Inquiry Training Model	Hilda Taba Richard Suchman	Designed primarily for development of inductive mental processes and academic reasoning or theory building, but these capacities are useful for personal and social goals as well.
Science Inquiry Model	Joseph J. Schwab (also much of the Curriculum Reform Movement of the 1960s)	Designed to teach the research system of a discipline, but also expected to have effects in other domains (sociological methods may be taught in order to increase social understanding and social problem-solving).
Concept Attainment Model	Jerome Bruner	Designed primarily to develop inductive reasoning, but also for concept development and analysis.
Developmental Model	Jean Piaget Irving Sigel Edmund Sullivan	Designed to increase general intellectual development, especially logical reasoning, but can be applied to social and moral development as well (see Kohlberg, 1966).
Advance Organizer Model	David Ausubel	Designed to increase the efficiency of information processing capacities to meaningfully absorb and relate bodies of knowledge.

Figure 1A. *The Information Processing Family of Models.*

Making Theories Practical

We did not make up the models of teaching you will learn here, nor did we invent the theories upon which they are based. Most of these ideas have been available to educators for many years. Our contribution has been to develop a way of making these theories operational, and to describe what teachers *do* when they teach according to one theory or another.

To translate a theory into practical teaching form, we employ a set of four concepts: *syntax*, *principles of reaction*, *social system*, and *support system*. The first two concepts are especially important in making a theory practical.

Syntax describes the model as a flow of actions. If teachers were to use the model, how would they begin? What would they do first, second, third? We describe syntax in terms of sequences of events, which we call *phases*. Each model has a distinct *flow* of phases—for example, present material to the learner, develop confronting situation—or, present organizing ideas to students, provide data sources. A comparison of the structural phasing of models reveals the practical differences

Model	Major Theorist	Mission or Goals for Which Most Applicable
Group Investigation Model	Herbert Thelen John Dewey	Development of skills for participation in democratic social process through combined emphasis on interpersonal (group) skills and academic-inquiry skills. Aspects of personal development are important outgrowths of this model.
Classroom Meeting Model (Social Problem-Solving)	William Glasser	Development of self-understanding and responsibility to oneself and one's social group.
Social Inquiry Model	Byron Massialas Benjamin Cox	Social problem-solving, primarily through academic inquiry and logical reasoning.
Laboratory Method Model	National Training Laboratory (NTL), Bethel, Maine	Development of interpersonal and group skills and, through this, personal awareness and flexibility.
Jurisprudential Model	Donald Oliver James P. Shaver	Designed primarily to teach the jurisprudential frame of reference as a way of thinking about and resolving social issues.
Role Playing Model	Fannie Shaftel George Shaftel	Designed to induce students to inquire into personal and social values, with their own behavior and values becoming the source of their inquiry.
Social Simulation Model	Sarene Boocock	Designed to help students experience various social processes and realities and to examine their own reactions to them.

Figure 1B. *The Social Family of Models.*

among them. An inductive strategy has a different phase and a different sequence than a deductive one.

Principles of reaction guide the teacher's responses to the learner; they tell the teacher how to regard the learner and respond to what he or she does. In some models, the teacher overtly tries to shape behavior by rewarding certain student activities and maintaining a neutral stance toward others. In other models, such as those designed to develop creativity, the teacher tries to maintain a nonevaluative, carefully equal stance so that the learners become self-directing. Principles of reaction provide the teacher with rules of thumb by which to "tune in" to the student and select appropriate responses to what the student does.

The social system provides a description of student and teacher roles and relationships and the kinds of norms that are encouraged. The leadership roles of the

Model	Major Theorist	Mission or Goals for Which Most Applicable
Nondirective Model	Carl Rogers	Emphasis on building the capacity for personal development in terms of self-awareness, understanding, autonomy, and self-concept.
Awareness Training Model	Fritz Perls	Increasing one's capacity for self-exploration and self-awareness. Much emphasis on development of inter-personal awareness and understanding, as well as body and sensory awareness.
Synectics Model	William Gordon	Personal development of creativity and creative problem-solving.
Conceptual Systems Model	David Hunt	Designed to increase personal complexity and flexibility.

Figure 1C. *The Personal Family of Models.*

teacher vary greatly from model to model. In some models, the teacher is a reflector or a facilitator of group activity; in others, a counselor of individuals; and in still others, a taskmaster. The concept of hierarchical relationships is explained in terms of the sharing of initiating activity by teacher and learner, the location of authority, and the amount of control over activity that emerges from the process of interaction. In some models, the teacher is the center of activity and the source of input — the organizer and pacer of the situation. Some models provide for relatively equal distribution of activity between teacher and student, whereas others place the student at the center. Finally, different models reward different student behaviors. In some, the students are rewarded for completing a job done or sticking to a prescribed line of inquiry; in others, the students' reward is knowing that they have learned something.

One way to describe a teaching model, then, is in terms of the degree of structure in the learning environment. That is, as roles, relationships, norms, and activities become less externally imposed and more within the student's control, the social system becomes less structured.

The support system refers to additional requirements beyond the usual human skills, capacities, and technical facilities necessary to implement a model. For example, a human relations model may require a trained leader; a nondirective model may require a particular type of personality (exceedingly patient and supportive). If a model postulates that students teach themselves, with the role of the teacher limited to consultation and facilitation, what support is necessary? A classroom supplied only with textbooks would be limiting and prescriptive; additional support in the form of books, films, self-instructional systems, travel arrangements, and the like is necessary. Support requirements are derived from two sources: the role specifications for the teacher and the substantive demands of the experience.

Those of you who have used our *Models of Teaching* text will notice that some descriptions of the model in the present book are slightly different from those in the earlier work. This is because, as we worked with different models, we gained greater ability to describe them and could incorporate more elements of the theory of a model into its basic set of activities. Therefore, we are now more precise about the events that take place within any given phase of activity. Occasionally, we have revised or expanded the phases of activity. In all cases, we are able to identify specific planning and teaching skills that facilitate the implementation of a model. We have learned and changed over the years!

Although we are delighted with our increased ability to describe initial teacher (and student) behaviors for each model, and although we feel this will greatly enhance easy and early mastery of each model, we offer a caution to our supporters, and to our critics. A model of teaching is not a simple fixed formula for completing a job. It provides definite ideas for creating an environment from which students are likely to learn certain kinds of things, but it has to become a flexible, fluid instrument that is modified to fit different types of subject matter and that responds to students who are different from one another.

There is an old saying that fencing coaches preach to their students: Treat the sword like a bird. If you hold it too tightly, you choke it! If you hold it too loosely, it will fly away! So it is with a model of teaching. If one uses it too rigidly, it becomes a blunt instrument. If one holds it too lightly, it dissolves and becomes undistinguishable from any other method of teaching. It fails to do its work!

Experience and Research with Models

Our impression from experience is that in-service teachers learn models of teaching that are new to them somewhat more easily and rapidly than do teachers-in-training or inexperienced teachers. This is probably because experienced teachers have more of the general competencies of teaching in hand and are more comfortable working with children during the first stages of practice with a new teaching approach.

In a series of research studies, we asked the question: How does the "natural" teaching style of teachers affect their ability to learn new models of teaching? The answer to this appears to be that teachers of nearly any style can master any of the models of teaching identified above with relatively little difficulty. Not everyone learns every model equally well or needs to use any given model regularly. However, nearly all teachers are capable of mastering the fundamentals of several models of teaching and of applying them effectively in the classroom.

Teachers very definitely have preferences for different models and use some more than others. We believe, however, that a range of approaches is needed. Once this is accepted, teachers who attempt to widen their repertoire will discover delights in some models of teaching that at first seemed unattractive.

Generally speaking, the time needed to learn new models of teaching shortens with each new acquisition. It takes several, perhaps five or six trials, for a teacher to be able to comfortably handle unfamiliar models in the classroom at first, but fewer trials are needed with each successive model.

Over the years, we have conducted a series of investigations into how people acquire and use models of teaching that are new to them. At this point, we believe that most of us first learn a model in a form appropriate for short lessons or units.

This "short form" is relatively rigid: we "follow the steps" (phases) of the model rather closely during the first practice sessions. With increasing practice, we learn to transform the model and expand it, adapting it to the kinds of things that we teach best, to the children being taught, and to the local conditions. In time, we learn to apply the model more effectively to curriculum materials and to combine it with other models of teaching, thereby incorporating it into the working repertoire. Following that, we gradually learn to teach the model to the children, helping them to make the model their own as part of their quest to "learn how to learn." For example, in science classes we help students learn to carry on inductive inquiry by themselves, our function as teachers becoming one of helping them learn rather than one of leading them through a sequence of learning steps.

To reiterate, the stages of mastering a model are: (1) learning how to apply it in some acceptable form; (2) expanding, embellishing, and transforming it to our own styles and curriculum; (3) applying its elements to the roles we play in our classroom; (4) combining it with other models; and (5) teaching it to the children themselves.

Some people quickly grasp the essential ideas and procedures of a model after reading brief introductory materials and viewing or experiencing a demonstration. We have found that approximating the sequence of activities of a model—its syntax —is not difficult in most cases. However, implementing a model in a way that truly reflects its theoretical underpinnings and fulfills all its potential objectives requires a deeper understanding. Consequently, we have chosen to err on the side of specificity in the explanation in our training systems. Some teachers, maybe most teachers, will not need the extent of explanation, illustration, and step-by-step training that our systems offer. They may be turned off by what is perceived as prescription. However, other teachers we have worked with prefer a highly structured training approach with many illustrations and examples.

We hope you do not take our effort to provide as much detail as we can as a belief that there is only one way to learn new models of teaching (or only one way to teach them). Our primary purpose, rather, is to provide something for everyone, something for an audience representing all grade levels, subject matter, and learning styles! When you feel ready to move on to the next steps in training, by all means do so. (We shall speak more about learning options later in this introduction).

Expanded Uses of a Model

We have mentioned that the goal in the initial stage of training (and throughout our training systems) is for teachers to use a model to develop short lessons, and to try these out several times with colleagues and small groups of students. The ultimate uses of a model extend far beyond the construction of the relatively short, isolated lessons that conveniently serve the training function.

A model can be used to guide learning activities extended over a long period of time, to diagnose and evaluate pupils, and to train students to use the model independently. Teachers can create many variations on each model, or they can take the "essence" of a model, dropping the syntax and phases, and perceptively use the key elements in an impromptu learning situation. Models can be designed into learning materials, and thereby become materials-mediated instead of teacher-mediated. (Programmed instruction, for example, is designed around Skinner's work.)

The models of teaching we present in these three books are applicable to all types of learning settings, both traditional and open. In open environments, self-directed, materials-mediated learning activities can be developed by designing them around the phases of the model. Students can work with one another, using key elements of the model. Bulletin boards can be based on one or more models of teaching. Learning centers can be developed around different models of teaching. For example, there can be an Inquiry Corner—or, alternatively, a Science Corner—that is based on the Inquiry Training Model. There can be a Concept Corner where students acquire concepts for many subject areas through concept attainment activities.

We touch on these expanded uses briefly in the last portion of each instructional system, but we do not train directly for them. We strongly urge small groups of teachers to brainstorm regarding the adaptation of models to different learning settings.

TRAINING TO LEARN A MODEL

The three books in this series are designed to help present and future teachers teach themselves a variety of models of teaching. One book presents teaching models from the information processing family; another presents models from the social family; and another, models from the personal family.

The Training Approach: Four Components

In these books, the materials for each model have been organized into four components: I) Describing and Understanding the Model; II) Viewing the Model; III) Planning and Peer Teaching; and IV) Adapting the Model. This organization reflects our belief about how one goes about training individuals to learn a complex performance behavior such as teaching (or tennis or computer programming or flying).

The notion is quite simple. First, you will read or hear a verbal description of the new model; this will give a general overview of the major operations and an explanation of the rationale, or theory, behind the activities included in the model. You need to become familiar with the goals of the model—that is, what its activities can and cannot accomplish—and with its key ideas. For example, if you were learning tennis, you would need to know at the onset that there are forehand shots, backhand shots, serves, lobs, and net play. You would also have to know something about scoring and about when the objective of the activity is accomplished—that is, about "games," "sets," and "matches." Learning a model of teaching is like learning to play tennis; at first, then, you would need a description of the activity—its objectives and key features. Component I of each model provides this.

Many of us prefer to see a demonstration of the activity. Demonstrations make words come alive, especially if the new activity is unfamiliar to us. So, in training for a model of teaching we move next to a demonstration, the model in action. In these learning systems, demonstration is accomplished through annotated transcripts of actual teaching sessions and/or through the optional use of audio tapes of lessons. In Component II of these models, you will find a transcript of a demonstration of the model, which we refer to as the *demonstration transcript.* In addition, you may have available a demonstration audio tape. In the exercises and activities, we shall be referring primarily to the demonstration transcript, but other forms of demonstration could also be used, or someone skilled in the model could conduct a live demonstration.

Finally, we practice. In tennis, you hit balls against a backboard or return "shots" from a ball-machine, spending hours, first on the forehand and then on the backhand, gradually learning more and more about the discrepancy between what you are doing and a *good* stroke. Similarly, in learning a model of teaching, you study and practice the *major elements* of a model several times before actually playing a game. Aspects of the theory are further explained and opportunity to apply your knowledge of them is provided through written exercises.

In Component III, it is time to move from practice to the "court." In teaching, this means planning and teaching an actual lesson. In tennis, it means playing one or two games at a time—not an entire match! In teaching, we select a topic, shape it according to the model, plan lessons, and teach them to a group of peers. Peer teaching is different from practice with children and has advantages over such practice when we are just trying out a model, namely that adult "learners" can coach us as we practice. Peer teaching gives us a chance to master the elements of the model before we try it with children, so that we are more surefooted when we do work with them.

After peer teaching, we suggest that you try the model with children, preferably small groups, but perhaps classroom-size groups. Again, these trials should be relatively short lessons or sets of lessons. Remember, at this point you are just sharpening your skills. (It is important to master the basics of your own tennis game before figuring out how to defend against such players as Chris Evert, Jimmy Connors, or Arthur Ashe! Or before learning how to play on different types of courts, such as grass, clay, and asphalt.) Mastering the basics comes before working out your own personal style, which surely will develop and be unique to you even though the model remains the same.

Finally, with the basic skills and activities in place, it is time to explore the model in the context of your actual teaching situation, your curriculum, and your students. It's time to think about the long-term goals of the model—for yourself, your subject area, and your students. You ask questions such as: How do I take the materials and curriculums I work with and enhance them with the model? How do I teach students to use a model over a long period of time? How do I develop variations on the basic model or incorporate elements of it into my style? How can I "stretch" a model so that it's not a cookie-cutter, thirty-minute lesson, but instead becomes a paradigm for many days and weeks of learning activities? How do I move from using the model of teaching as a guide for a short lesson to using it as guidelines for larger curricular sequences and, finally, for organizing the classroom as a learning environment? These questions are covered in Component IV, Adapting the Model.

In summary, the written materials (and the audio-visual materials, if available) are designed to help you 1) master the theory and basic elements of a model (describing and understanding the model), 2) provide demonstration (viewing the model), 3) initiate practice (planning and peer teaching), and 4) extend the model to your classroom setting and curricular planning (adapting the model). These components and their parts are listed in Figure 2.

COMPONENT I: DESCRIBING AND UNDERSTANDING THE MODEL

Materials	Activity
1. Theory and Overview	Reading
2. Theory in Practice	Reading
3. Taking Theory Into Action	Reading/Writing
4. Theory Checkup	Writing

COMPONENT II: VIEWING THE MODEL

Materials	Activity
1. Analyzing Teaching	Reading/Writing
2. Viewing the Lesson	Reading/Writing/Discussion

Optional Material	Optional Activity
3. Analyzing the Demonstration	Discussion/Writing

COMPONENT III: PLANNING AND PEER TEACHING

Materials	Activity
1. Selecting the Topic	Reading/Writing
2. Preparing and Organizing Materials	Reading/Writing
3. Determining Educational Objectives	Reading/Writing
4. Completing the Planning Guide	Writing
5. Peer Teaching	Teaching
6. Analyzing the Lesson	Discussion/Analysis

Optional Material	Optional Activity
7. Microteaching and Analysis	Teaching/Analysis

COMPONENT IV: ADAPTING THE MODEL

Materials	Activity
1. Curriculum Transformation	Reading
2. Long-Term Uses	Reading
3. Combining the Model With Other Models of Teaching	Reading

Figure 2. *Components of the Training System.*

Ways to Go Through the Training System: Options

We have provided options for two reasons: teachers differ in their learning styles and preferences, and training situations differ in their organizational possibilities, flexibility, and support systems. The major training options are three. They concern:

1. the sequence and order of components
2. the medium for demonstration of the model: written transcript, live, audio-filmstrip, or photostrip
3. the role of the trainer: self-instructional, group instruction with instructor as facilitator, and instructor-led presentations

Essentially, the material is self-instructional: you can work through it on your own (except for peer teaching), or with a group of colleagues. An instructor is not necessary. On the other hand, a knowledgeable instructor can greatly enhance the learning situation by serving as a facilitator and reactor. Our preference is for teachers to work in groups, selecting the models they wish to concentrate on and helping one another master them. However, the material can form the basis for pre-planned workshops in which all participants study the same models.

Although this series is designed so that one first learns the theory of the model, then analyzes demonstrations of it, then practices it with peers, and finally practices it in the classroom, there are many alternative sequences, all equally viable. Some groups prefer to begin with demonstration. These people would like to see the model before they read about it. This makes perfectly good sense. In other groups, the beginning activity might be to appoint one teacher to demonstrate the model live with children or with those being trained. This requires that the demonstrator master the theory, read the transcript lesson, and practice the model so that he or she can introduce the training with the live demonstration. It is also possible to begin with curriculum materials, analyzing them to find which model of teaching is most appropriate and then concentrating on learning how to adapt the model to the curriculum materials. For example, most approaches to the teaching of reading are built upon a particular model of teaching or the combination of a few of them. Teachers of reading may prefer to begin with the models that underlie the curriculums they are using. For most of us, the "understanding first" sequence is the most comfortable (see Figure 3).

Many of us can handle abstract ideas only after we have experienced the concrete situation. We also do not like to perfect isolated skills without seeing the whole; we find that it's easier to go back to the task of mastering the basics when we have seen an example of the end product! For those who prefer a quick overview and then need to see a model of the activity before going further in training, we suggest another sequence. Figure 4 indicates a way of meeting these needs.

Some people (not the authors) like to go right to the tennis match before learning anything about the game. That is another alternative. It is possible to view a filmstrip and/or read the demonstration transcript before undertaking the Overview and Theory into Practice Steps (see Figure 5).

Flexibility in developing the training sequence will depend, of course, on

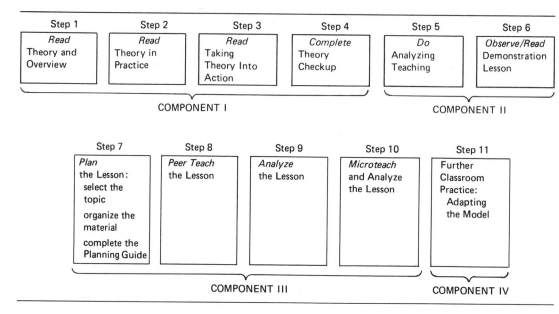

Figure 3. *The "Understanding First" Approach.*

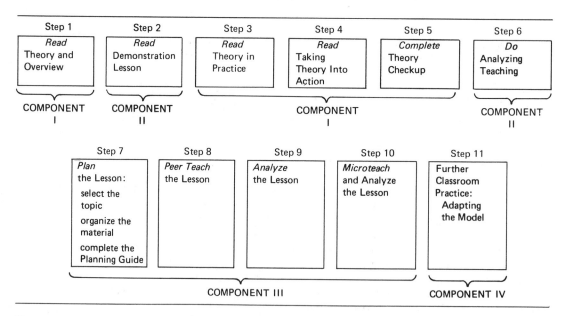

Figure 4. *"A Quick Overview and the Real Thing" Approach.*

whether the materials are used on an individualized or an instructor-directed basis. However, we do want to alert both instructors and trainees that alternatives are possible!

In the early years of our work with models of teaching, we used to spend weeks of instruction on a single model, going deeply into the theory, the issues in the particular field of knowledge, and our own and our students' personal philosophy of education. Besides believing that these considerations were important for our students, we believed they were necessary for performance mastery. What we have learned in recent years is that initial training in a model can take place in a relatively short period of time—perhaps four to five hours from introduction through peer teaching. Teachers are quick to sense their own problems and correct their behavior. In the first planning and peer teaching sessions, they note their points of confusion. For clarification, they go back to the training materials, to their instructor, or to their colleagues. After that, it is *practice* and *more practice*! What teachers need is time to absorb the ideas, to master the skills, and to try out the model with many topics and pupils.

Discussions of the philosophy of learning and teaching underlying particular models, and questions concerning specific difficulties in applying the model in the classroom are more valid and are dealt with more meaningfully following some degree of practice with the model. This is less true with experienced teachers than with preservice students. Even so, we strongly advise *everyone* to get into practice as soon as possible. It has been amazing to us how much a satisfactory learning experience alters initial questions, concerns, and doubts, regardless of previous experience.

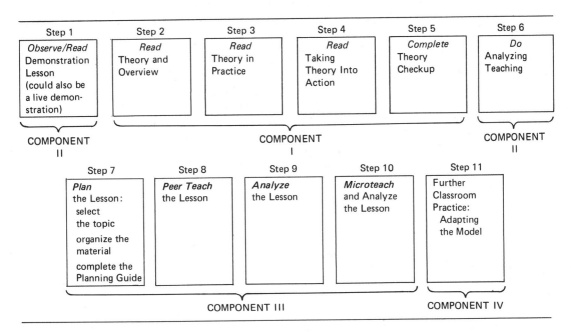

Figure 5. *"See the Real Thing First and Find Out Later" Approach.*

Everyone feels some insecurity in learning a new skill; however, we can almost promise that in four or five hours of earnest work, you will have enough initial competence in a model to, first, feel comfortable about your own strength and skill, and, second, to correct problem areas on your own and polish and shape the model in your own style!

This system is aimed almost exclusively at developing *initial clinical* (or performance) competence in a model. Although the overview materials discuss the philosophical and theoretical rationale for the model, we have not designed these materials to explore very many of the interesting issues surrounding these theories. We can imagine instructors supplementing practice in a model with readings and discussions on the philosophical, theoretical, or even empirical background and issues of a model.

Analysis of Teaching

One of the features of this training is the constant analysis of teaching that is included. We regard the analysis of teaching, not as an evaluation of teacher performance, but as a *feedback* tool, one that enables teachers to obtain reasonably objective information about their performance of the model of teaching and that provides guidelines for modifying teaching activities the next time.

In our training system, teaching analysis is introduced in the demonstration component. We have developed a Teaching Analysis Guide for each model that covers the major activities and principles of reaction for the phases in that model. The Guides usually consist of between fifteen and twenty questions and are first used in conjunction with the demonstration lessons. A more important use comes during peer teaching, when feedback is based on the Guide. A sample portion of a Teaching Guide appears in Figure 6.

The Guide is divided according to the phases of the model with a scale for analyzing important activites in each phase. Because every teaching situation is (and should be) sufficiently unpredictable that different teaching behaviors are necessary, we cannot be exact in measuring just how well any given teaching situation turns out; hence, the scale. We have grown more and more committed to the idea that once teachers have mastered the basics of a model, they should transpose and transform it, so that every model assumes a variety of forms. Thus, measuring competence and providing feedback should be flexible. There are standards of performance, but good performance appears in many forms. The Guide tells where to look for the essential competencies of each model and provides latitude so that different forms of competence can be identified.

Skills in Teaching

Two terms that you will come across in these books are *skill* (teaching skill) and *move*, by which we mean a particular teaching behavior that contributes to the effectiveness and uniqueness of that model. Asking a higher-order question, paraphrasing a student's comment, and summarizing the major points of a discussion are examples of teaching moves or skills. Sometimes a teaching skill is a single teacher comment or question, and sometimes it is a series of comments or questions.

During the course of a model or any thirty- or forty-minute learning activity,

PHASE TWO: Testing Concept Attainment

12. After the concept was agreed upon, did the teacher present additional exemplars and ask whether they contained the concept?	Thoroughly	Partially	Missing	Not Needed
13. Did the teacher ask the students to justify their answers?	Thoroughly	Partially	Missing	Not Needed
14. Were the students able to supply their own exemplars to fit the concept?	Thoroughly	Partially	Missing	Not Needed
15. Did the teacher ask the students to justify their exemplars by identifying the essential attributes?	Thoroughly	Partially	Missing	Not Needed

PHASE THREE: Analyzing Strategies

16. Did the teacher ask the students to describe the thinking processes they used in attaining the concept?	Thoroughly	Partially	Missing	Not Needed
17. Did the teacher ask the students to reflect on the role of attributes and concepts in their thinking strategies?	Thoroughly	Partially	Missing	Not Needed
18. Did the teacher ask the students to evaluate the effectiveness of their strategies?	Thoroughly	Partially	Missing	Not Needed

Figure 6. *Part of a Teaching Analysis Guide.*

the teacher (and students) exhibit hundreds of behaviors and many skills. Some models are dependent on how we master particular teacher skills. We have tried to identify and describe these skills. In addition to *interactive* teaching skills, we have identified critical *planning* skills. Some training approaches separate planning and teaching skills from teaching strategies. We prefer to introduce skills as part of the models and teach them in the context of the model, where the phases of activities provide guidelines as to when and how to use a particular skill.

WHAT IS IN THIS SYSTEM AND HOW TO USE IT

There are three books in this series. They cover description and understanding, demonstration, planning and peer teaching, and adaptation for models in the information processing, social, and personal families. Within each family, the models dealt with are:

Information Processing Family
        Concept Attainment Model(s)
        Inquiry Training Model
        Advance Organizer Model

Social Family
>   Jurisprudential Model
>   Simulation Model
>   Role Playing Model

Personal Family
>   Synectics Model
>   Nondirective Model

We repeat that these materials are designed to be used on a self-instructional basis, usually in a student-directed group with the instructor serving as a facilitator. We strongly urge that teachers share their learning of a model with one another. It's usually richer, more instructive, and more fun that way.

Component I:
Describing and Understanding the Model

The first of the four components of our training approach is Describing and Understanding the Model. This component consists of two readings and a Theory Checkup. The first reading (Theory and Overview) discusses the goals, assumptions, key ideas, and procedures (syntax) of the model. The second reading (Taking Theory Into Action) provides further discussion and illustration of the model's major concepts. Through short written exercises, you are given opportunities to apply these concepts and to identify any difficulties you may have. We have made a special effort to select the major ideas you will apply when you teach and to develop a strong training sequence for them. It is one thing to read about an idea in the overview and another to practice and apply it. We urge you to concentrate especially on this reading and to do so at the point in the training sequence that is the most appropriate for you.

Finally, the Theory Checkup enables you to check your understanding of the ideas discussed and illustrated in the three previous readings. The checkup is for your use only; it is not a test. If you did not grasp an item, you may want to re-read the relevant pages in the readings. Some people may want to complete the Theory Checkup after the first reading; others may want to wait until they have finished the second reading. One way to view the checkup is as a guide to tell you what to concentrate on. It can also be viewed as a means of checking your understanding before going on to Components II and III. No doubt you will be better prepared for the Theory Checkup after you complete the second reading.

Component II: Viewing the Model

Component II (Viewing the Model) includes two learning activities. The first is reading the Teaching Analysis Guide and identifying any items that you do not understand. The second activity is reading the demonstration transcript. As you read the lesson, your attention is directed to the occurrence of the phases of the model. We suggest that you share your spontaneous reactions and comments with the group.

One thing to keep in mind is that there is no such thing as a "perfect" model.

There are always ways to enrich the lesson, or to improve a particular aspect. Besides, each of us have our preferred styles and expressions, which have nothing to do with the model per se. We have tried to select demonstrations that reveal the phases of the model and the major elements discussed in the text. Sometimes this does not happen, even in demonstration lessons. One of your jobs as an observer is to comment on those places in the lesson that may deviate (either by commission or omission) from your understanding of the model up to that point. Besides being critical, we'd like you to be attuned to the strengths of the lessons, the teacher moves that were particularly strong, the way the topic and material were designed for the model, and the way the lesson was organized for presentation. If there is time, you may want to read the model a second time, using the Teaching Analysis Guide as a format for analysis. Optional activities are included for use with audio tapes, where available, or with live demonstrations.

Component III: Planning and Peer Teaching

The activities in this component will guide you through the steps in planning a model lesson, which you will then peer teach to a small group of colleagues. The planning steps include topic selection, designing and organizing materials, and selecting behavioral objectives. Each step is discussed in terms of its unique features for the particular model you are studying. Special planning skills are taught in this part of the training program. A Planning Guide is provided to assist you in completing the various aspects of planning and to alert you to problem areas. Sample planning forms are provided for some of the models. In some cases, materials are provided from which to develop peer teaching lessons, in the event that you want to teach from them rather than use them as guides or suggestions. (Component IV also includes curriculum materials from which lessons may be planned.) We strongly urge you to select your own topics and prepare your own materials. This is one of the best ways to apply the ideas of the model and test your planning skills.

Peer teaching is just what the name suggests. It means that teachers practice teaching skills or models of teaching in groups, taking turns playing the role of the learners. Peer teaching accomplishes several things. First, it enables you to practice a new teaching strategy before you try it out with students. This gives you a chance to familiarize yourself with the structure of the model, to become more comfortable with it as you work it out in the classroom. It provides practice, not only in the actual teaching, but also in the planning for it. Translating material into new and unfamiliar models of teaching requires you to think differently about your teaching than you may have done before, and you need practice to become comfortable with the new approaches and moves.

A second benefit of peer teaching is that, because you do it with one another, you gain the kinds of feedback that fellow professional teachers can give. If a half-dozen teachers are practicing the same model and take turns teaching it, you can coach one another. Often, when you are in the role of student you see things that you do not see when you are in the role of teacher. Thus, you can avail yourselves of one another's professional opinion and coaching.

Third, peer teaching gets people working together to improve their classroom performance. It increases dialogue about the dynamics of teaching, gives a language for discussing the problems of teaching, and provides a warm and enriching experience in itself. Also, when you teach with others, you add their ideas to your own. When you see four or five people teaching the same model that you are trying to learn, you are exposed to new ideas about variations on that model, and so your learning is richer.

Being a Teacher in Peer Teaching. When you plan a lesson for your peers, you should plan one for their level. That is, you should select material that will be stimulating for your colleagues. This does not mean that you cannot select material that is also appropriate for children. Many concepts in mathematics, science, social science, and literature are fun for adults to learn again, especially when you see them highlighted by a fresh approach. Because of the constraints of time, most peer teaching lessons have to be relatively short—they are simulations of the kind of teaching we do with children. Make sure that there is enough time both to be taught and to provide feedback. Talk through your planning before beginning the model, describe the materials you are going to use, and be certain that everyone is oriented to the lesson.

Being a Learner in Peer Teaching. As learners in peer teaching, you should be yourselves. The best way to kill peer teaching is to "act the role of the child." You should permit yourselves to be engaged by your fellow teachers as you would if they were teaching a course or workshop, or engaging in any other kind of learning activity. However, not only are you learners to the teacher, but you are also learning yourselves, and you need to be in a position to provide feedback and coaching to the one who teaches. Thus, you need to familiarize yourselves thoroughly with the model before you begin, and perhaps to have copies of the Teaching Analysis Guide so that you can analyze the teaching as it goes along, in preparation for the feedback session.

Being an Observer in Peer Teaching. In a group of five or six, it is wise for one person to be the teacher, three or four to be the learners, and one person simply to assume the role of observer. The observer uses the Teaching Guide and should be in charge of the feedback session, helping the teacher analyze the teaching process and drawing from the learners their opinions and insights about what went on. In most cases the observer becomes the leader of the post-mortem.

Organizing the Peer Teaching. It is our experience that the most comfortable size for a peer teaching group is between five and seven. With that size, there are enough people to play the role of learner, someone is available to be observer, and the group is large enough to provide diverse opinions, yet small enough to conduct its business in a relatively short period of time. Optimally, the six or seven people are all studying the same model of teaching, learning the theory, viewing the demonstrations, and then taking turns as teachers in a series of peer teaching activities. If this is the case, then before each individual tries out the teaching with children, she or he will have taught the model at least once and seen it taught a half-dozen times. By the end of that period of time, they should all begin to feel extremely comfortable with the model and well aware of the role of the learner. One of the most artful aspects of learning the new model of teaching is to "feel" what the learners feel when they are introduced to the model. The more we can anticipate how children will react, the more we can prepare ourselves for their reactions and ease their way into the new role required by the model.

Microteaching. The last activity in the planning and peer teaching component is to teach the lesson to a small group of students—what we call microteaching. We recommend that you make an audio tape of your microteaching session, so that alone, or with colleagues, you can review the lesson, using the Teaching Analysis Guide.

Component IV: Adapting the Model

The major purpose of this component is to present ways of adapting the model for long-term use in the classroom. We discuss how to incorporate existing curriculum materials by including samples of elementary and secondary texts and showing how the models can provide new approaches to them. We also discuss long-term goals with respect to the development of pupil skills and teacher skills. In addition, we offer a few ideas we may have for "stretching the model" or distilling its essence. In other words, we share our notions about moving away from sequential phases and toward applying elements of the model in a dynamic, ongoing instructional context. The third section in this component covers suggestions for combining the model with other models of teaching.

The major organizational decisions that trainees and/or instructors will need to anticipate during training are summarized in Figure 7.

Tips to the Instructor:
Some Ways to Simplify the Training System

1. Provide more direct instruction and less self-directed reading. For example, in Component I (Describing and Understanding the Model), assign the first reading (Theory and Overview) for the students to read on their own. Plan to teach the ideas in the second reading (Taking Theory into Action) in a lecture-recitation session, using the materials and exercises from the section.
2. Review the syntax of the models at the different stages of instruction.
3. Augment the demonstration transcript with a live demonstration of your own. This will give the students an opportunity to experience the model directly as a learner before planning and peer teaching.

COMPONENT I: DESCRIBING AND UNDERSTANDING THE MODEL

1. The order in which the readings should be covered.
2. How much, if any, discussion to have about the material in Component I.

COMPONENT II: VIEWING THE MODEL

1. Reading the model individually *or* as a group.
2. Whether to observe a live demonstration, read the demonstration transcript, or hear a taped lesson.
3. Whether to analyze the demonstration lesson using the Teaching Analysis Guide, and if so, how to organize groups to do this.
4. Whether to see several live demonstrations in addition to the demonstration transcript.

COMPONENT III: PLANNING AND PEER TEACHING

1. Allow time for planning; provide feedback.
2. Organize and schedule small groups for peer teaching.
3. Arrange for microteaching. If possible, video-tape or audio-tape the lesson. Obtain the equipment.
4. Analyze the microteaching lesson, alone or with someone. Obtain equipment, either video tape or audio tape.

COMPONENT IV: ADAPTING THE MODEL

1. Whether a group discussion and/or learning activity should be developed around this component.

Figure 7. *A Summary of Organizational Decisions for the Trainee and/or Instructor.*

THE MODELS IN THIS BOOK

There are two models of teaching in the personal family, Synectics and Nondirective Teaching. These models share a focus on the development of human potential. Synectics concentrates on the development of creativity; the Nondirective strategy is concerned with the development of emotional awareness and capacity.

The personal family of models differs from the information processing family in several important ways. First, the content of the instruction is the personal experiences and feelings of the students, rather than an external body of knowledge. This content is highly subjective and unique to each student. There are no standard answers to questions—answers depend on the individual's frame of reference. Second, the goals of instruction in the personal family are not the same for all students. People differ in their capacity for creativity and in their stages of personal growth. Each student must be seen on his or her own terms.

The models in the personal family also differ from the models in the social family, primarily in the role of the group. Goals related to the larger society or social group are not prominent in the personal family; the goals here are much more individualistic and idiosyncratic. Personal growth is the direct goal, although social growth may occur as a result. The social group does not modify or greatly influence the reality of the individual in this family. In this sense, the larger social world—how individuals interact and perceive others and how they are perceived by them—does not figure prominently in the instructional process of this family, as it does in the social family.

William Gordon developed Synectics as a strategy for improving the creative problem-solving ability of industrial engineers. He bases his strategy on the use of metaphoric activity. Gordon's assumptions about the creative process and his attempt to *teach* people how to be more creative are fairly unorthodox. Traditionally, creativity has been regarded as an innate talent, something we cannot teach or influence directly. Like Concept Attainment, Synectics has two variations—

two similar but distinct models of teaching. One model (Creating Something New) is designed to help students see familiar ideas, situations, or problems in new, more creative ways. The other variation (Making the Strange Familiar) uses metaphoric activity to make unfamiliar material more meaningful. Synectics can be used in many content areas, and as a means of linking ideas across content areas. The outcomes from this model vary tremendously. They range from a piece of creative writing and the design for a new product to the solution to an interpersonal problem and the increased capacity for empathy.

Nondirective Teaching is based on Carl Rogers' early work in therapeutic counseling. The model develops the role of the teacher as a counselor or facilitator who helps individual students perceive themselves and grow on their own terms. Rogers believes that each person has the capacity to grow and that teachers can trust the individual to guide his or her own growth.

The Nondirective Model we present here is designed primarily for a one-to-one relationship, although the principles and skills of Nondirective Teaching can be used to conduct group discussions oriented toward personal growth. The problems that are dealt with in this model can be personal, interpersonal, or academic. Finally, we discuss the application of Rogerian principles to the creation of classroom environments and organization. The open classroom and the use of learning contracts are examples of the student-centered education that Rogers advocates.

SYNECTICS MODEL

SCENARIO FOR THE SYNECTICS MODEL

A junior high school class is creating a book of short stories and poems. Their English teacher, Martin Abramowitz, has gradually become aware that the stories and poems, especially the poems, are hackneyed and ordinary. He feels that the project is going to fail. Surely there will be a product, a magazine that the class can share with parents and others in the school. But he thinks they could do much better. He has been helping individuals rewrite their poems and stories, and some of them have been improved, but on the whole he is disappointed with the class' work.

Then Abramowitz runs across the work of William Gordon of Cambridge, Massachusetts, who believes that creativity can be enhanced by a series of group exercises that help individuals to understand the process of creativity more completely and to use metaphors and analogies to "break set" and generate new alternatives. Abramowitz decides to try Gordon's methods. One morning, he has each of his students read a poem and a short story. He then says, "Today we're going to try something new that I hope will help us see our stories and poems in a different light. For the next fifteen or twenty minutes I want to play with ideas with you and then have you come back to your work and see what you can do to improve it. At the end of this exercise I'm going to ask you to rewrite part or all of your poems and stories." He begins by asking what a poem is. The children give a variety of answers, from which Abramowitz selects key words and writes them on the board:

"It doesn't have to rhyme."

"It lets your feelings come out."

"It uses different kinds of words."

He then asks, "How is a poem like an automobile?" The children are puzzled. Then one ventures, "It takes you on a trip. It's a word trip, and you have to have the road in your imagination."

Someone else says, "It is self-propelled—you just get in it and it goes."

Another student says, "When you're writing one, sometimes you have trouble getting the motor started."

After a time, Abramowitz says, "Pick an animal—any animal." The children suggest a variety of animals. He has them pick one. They select a giraffe. "Now," he asks, "how is a poem like a giraffe?"

"It has a lot of parts fastened together in funny ways," says one.

"It kind of stands above everything else and looks at things in a different way," says another.

The exercise goes on. After a time, Abramowitz asks the students to select one of the words that they have dealt with in discussing the poem. They select the word "above."

"How does it feel," he asks, "to be above?"

"You feel different," replies one. "You can see things you can't ordinarily see," says another.

"You'll start feeling superior if you don't watch out," says a third student.

And so it goes. Finally, Abramowitz asks the students to make lists of words that they have been dealing with that seem to be opposites in some ways, words that apply tension on one another. The students pick "giraffe" and "snail," for they feel that both are animals but that each is very different in the way it lives and works.

"Well," Abramowitz says, "let's come back to your poems and short stories. Think of them as giraffes and snails together; write your poems or stories as if they were a giraffe and a snail holding hands, going through the woods together."

Here are two of the products of that exercise.

The Motorcycle

It sounds like an enraged mountain lion.
It looks like a steel horse.
It shifts gear and changes notes.
It goes very fast.
The sound of the motorcycle
        breaks the stillness
            of the night.

The Adventures of Samual O'Brian, Secret Spy

It all happened when Samual Watkins O'Brian, an average blonde-haired thirty-five-year-old chemist, was working in Laboratory 200, Hartford, Connecticut for the government. While mixing chemicals in a beaker, the substance started glowing strangly. It also became very hot. At that moment he dropped it to the floor. He turned to run, but before he had time to take a step it crashed to the floor followed by a blinding explosion! As he started to run, he felt his skin shrinking. As he ran he shrank to a height of 5.5 inches, one tenth his normal height!!

His superior ran in with a fire extinguisher yelling, "What happened in here, Sam?"

While jumping up and down Sam yelled, "I've shrunk, I've shrunk!!" His superior made no reply. He again yelled out his cry for help. Then Sam, realizing that his yelling was useless over the roar of the fire that had now started, tugged at his superior's giant shoelace. His superior bent down to see what was happening with his shoelace and he saw a very very small and scared Samual O'Brian.

Samual yelled, "Hey Jack, pick me up CAREFULLY!"

His superior's reply was, "CRIPES! What happened to you?" Sam explained the story in Jack's ear while Jack ran swiftly with Sam in the palm of his hand to the guard on the second floor.

Jack said (when they got there), "Seal off the building! I have Top Secret government personnel and SPEED IT UP!!!!" Because of the excitement, Sam fainted.

The next thing he knew he was in the Central Security President's office, lying in a marble ashtray, filled with warm water (and plenty of bubbles, of course). He found himself staring into the face of David Shields, President of C.S.

Sam stated that he was so sorry to clutter up the President's desk but . . . . Then David broke in, "Oh, it's nothing, people shrink everyday around here, but I guess you wouldn't know because you can't see the rings around the bathtub. . . .er, uh, ashtray."

David presented Sam with a small box of cigars and a custom-fitted suit, James Bond style (if you know what I mean). Sam got dressed and David said, "We'd like you to work for us, Sam."

AN OUTLINE OF ACTIVITIES FOR THE SYNECTICS MODEL

Objectives	Materials	Activity

COMPONENT I: DESCRIBING AND UNDERSTANDING THE MODEL

Objectives	Materials	Activity
1. To recognize the goals, assumptions, and procedures of the Synectics Model.	Theory and Overview	Reading
2. To gain a sense of the model in action.	Theory in Practice	Reading
3. To recognize and use metaphoric activity.	Taking Theory Into Action	Reading/Writing
4. To evaluate your understanding of the Synectics Model.	Theory Checkup	Writing

COMPONENT II: VIEWING THE MODEL

Objectives	Materials	Activity
1. To become familiar with the Teaching Analysis Guide and identify items that you do not understand.	Teaching Analysis Guide	Reading
2. To identify phases of the model and comment on the lesson.	Demonstration Transcript	Reading/Writing/ Discussion
Optional: To apply the Teaching Analysis Guide to other demonstration lessons.	Live demonstration or televised lesson/Teaching Analysis Guide	Viewing/Group or Individual Analysis

COMPONENT III: PLANNING AND PEER TEACHING

Objectives	Materials	Activity
1. To select and formulate a topic and determine the mode of expression.	Choosing a Topic and Mode of Expression	Reading/Writing
2. To determine behavioral objectives for the peer teaching lesson.	Determining Educational Objectives	Reading/Writing
3. To prepare examples of stretching exercises and analogies.	Preparing Analogies and Stretching Exercises	Reading/Writing
4. To complete the Planning Guide for the Synectics Model.	Planning Guide	Reading/Writing
5. To peer teach the Synectics Model.	Three or four peers, analogies, exercises	Teaching
6. To analyze the Synectics lesson using the Teaching Analysis Guide.	Teaching Analysis Guide	Writing/Group Discussion or Individual Analysis
7. **Optional:** To teach the Synectics Model to a small group of students.	Small group of students, evocative questions, audio-cassette recorder, cassette	Teaching/Taping

AN OUTLINE OF ACTIVITIES FOR THE SYNECTICS MODEL

8. To analyze the microteaching lesson.   Teaching Analysis Guide   By self or in group/ Listen to audio recording and analyze the lesson.

COMPONENT IV: ADAPTING THE MODEL

1. To present alternative approaches for Synectic activities.   Curricular Possibilities and Adaptations   Reading

2. To plan the use of Synectics for long-term development of student creativity.   Long-Term Plans   Reading

3. To be aware of the possibilities of combining Synectics with other models of teaching.   Combining Synectics with other models of teaching   Reading

Component I

DESCRIBING
AND UNDERSTANDING
THE MODEL

THEORY AND OVERVIEW

William Gordon has developed procedures called Synectics to enhance the creativity of individuals. Most of us associate the creative process with the development of great works of art or music, or perhaps with a clever new invention. Gordon finds that the creative mechanism expressed through Synectics activities enhances empathetic ability, problem-solving capacity in regard to personal problems or social issues, and creative expression through writing. He also finds that the meaning of abstract ideas or concepts can be enhanced through creative activity.

There are two basic elements in the Synectics Model. The first element is metaphoric activity, which draws on an analogy or comparison. Gordon believes that metaphoric activity helps us "break set" in our thinking. The second element in this model is the function of the group as an integral part of the creative process. This use of metaphoric activity and the group to promote creativity is based on Gordon's rather unorthodox views on the nature of creativity and the role of metaphor in the creative process.

In this section we shall review Gordon's assumptions about creativity and his rationale for the use of metaphors. We shall discuss different states of creativity and introduce you to different types of metaphoric activity. Finally, we shall discuss two teaching strategies based on metaphoric activity.

As in some of the other models in this series, there are short exercises in this reading that we would like you to complete to help you apply your knowledge of the model.

Before you begin this reading, it may be interesting for you to recall your own assumptions about creativity and how to develop it in others. Later, you can compare these ideas with Gordon's views. Briefly list your own views here:

Assumptions About the Creative Process

Gordon begins with the important assumption that the creative process is not mysterious; it can be described, and it is possible to train persons to increase their creativity. Gordon's basic ideas about the creative process oppose conventional thinking about this subject. Traditionally, creativity is viewed as a mysterious, innate, and personal capacity that can be destroyed if its processes are probed too deeply. In contrast, Gordon believes that if individuals understand the psychological basis for the creative process, this basis can be used (1) to analyze the steps in creativity, (2) to promote greater creativity, and (3) to foster creativeness among group members. Gordon's view that creativity is enhanced by conscious behavior led him to describe creativity and to create training procedures that can be learned and applied in a variety of settings.

Gordon's second assumption is that creative invention in all fields—the arts, the sciences, engineering, and so forth—is similar, and is characterized by the same fundamental intellectual processes. This idea is contrary to the conventional belief that creativity in the arts is a special and mystical process that cannot be described or enhanced through training, and that is quite different from the process of creativity in the sciences and engineering. This discrimination can be seen in the choice of words that people use to describe the creative process. In the arts the word used to describe the process is creativity, whereas in engineering and the sciences it is invention. But if we look closely at the total work and creations of scientists, inventors, and artists, we see that the link between the arts and the sciences is much stronger than we often believe.

Gordon's third assumption is that the process by which an individual invents is directly analogous to the processes of group invention. Again, this is very different from the conventional view of creativity, which holds creativity to be an intensely personal experience that can be destroyed if it is probed too deeply. Because the creative process is so personal, we do not discuss it with students, nor do we ask how they formed their ideas. In addition, because the process is so personal, we feel that we should only teach information that is external to the process. As teachers, we feel, perhaps, that there is little that we can do to stimulate creativity directly. We can discuss forms of poetry, style, literary concepts, or the origin of inventions, but we can do little to stimulate the process of creativity. Since we view the creative process as personal, we can never move beyond consideration of the product into the creative process itself. In contrast, Gordon says that the group can work together to create, and that the process of creativity can be analyzed and used by the leader to promote greater creativity.

Gordon believes that the dynamics of the group speed the process of individual creativity. If this idea seems strange, think of the number of inventions or scientific discoveries that occur simultaneously. Recently, scientists at Stanford's Linear Accelerator, Stanford, California, and scientists at Brookhaven National Laboratory, Upton, New York, discovered subatomic psi particles. Common knowledge in the sciences often leads to simultaneous breakthroughs that greatly expand present theories or concepts. During periods of great creativity, artists often live together in communities supporting similar intellectual concepts, which are expressed through the medium of painting, writing, music, sculpture, or dance. Examples of such communities are the Impressionists in Paris, the Bloomsbury Group in London, and the Beat Generation in San Francisco and New York. The intent of the Synectics Model is to create in classrooms intellectual communities that are conducive to student creativity and exploration of new ideas in science, engineering, and the arts. Like Gordon, we are not denying that creativity is often an individual process and an individual response to a problem, but we do believe that the use of a certain set of procedures—in this case, Synectics—and the group process can facilitate individual creativity.

As we have just noted, the assumptions of the Synectics Model about creativity are different from traditional assumptions. Before we move onto a rationale for Synectics procedures, we want to summarize and compare these different views (see Figure 1). How do the assumptions of Synectics compare with your own views about creativity?

Traditional Views	**Nontraditional Views**
1. Creativity cannot be described. It is a mysterious, highly personal activity of individuals who have an innate capacity for creativity.	1. Creativity can be described. It can be enhanced by conscious attempts to promote the creative process in students.
2. Creativity in the arts is special. It is a mystical process that cannot be enhanced through training. It is different from the process of invention or hypothesis formulation in engineering and the sciences.	2. Creativity or invention in the arts, sciences, and engineering are similar, and are characterized by the same fundamental intellectual processes.
3. The process of creativity is individual, and cannot be duplicated by a group effort.	3. The process by which an individual creates is directly analogous to the way a group creates. In addition, a group using Synectics procedures can condense into several hours the processes that might take months for an individual working alone.

Figure 1. *Traditional and Nontraditional Views of Creativity.*

The Creative State and the Synectics Process

Synectics procedures are developed from an additional set of assumptions or hypotheses by Gordon about the psychology of the creative process. The first of these is that by bringing the creative process to consciousness and by developing conscious aids to creativity, we can increase the creativity capacity of individuals and groups. Directly teaching people a process of creativity will give them greater control over their actions and thus increase their ability to create. What we are looking for, then, is a set of procedures that can be taught to people.

A second assumption is that the "emotional component is more important than the intellectual, the irrational more important than the rational."[1] Gordon makes this assumption because he believes that nonrational interplay leaves room for open-ended thoughts that ultimately lead to a mental state in which new ideas are possible. In the end, however, the basis for decisions is always the rational. The irrational state is the best mental environment for exploring and expanding ideas, but it is not a decision-making state. Synectics does not undervalue the intellect; Gordon assumes that a basic technical competence is necessary to the formation of ideas. But he has found, as you will, that creativity is essentially an *emotional* process, one that requires elements of irrationality and emotion in order to capitalize on or enhance intellectual processes. Much of problem solving is rational and intellectual, but by adding the irrational we can enhance the creativity of the problem solving. The issue here is what set of procedures we can teach directly in order to bring out the irrational.

The third hypothesis is that the "emotional, irrational elements must be understood in order to increase the probability of success in a problem solving situation."[2] In other words, although the irrational is the key to creativity, it is assumed that the irrational and the emotional can be subject to analysis, and that this analysis can give the individual and the group the control over their irrationality and their emotionality that they need in order to increase their creativity. Just because creativity is partly irrational does not mean we have to abandon the idea of direct training for it, because, according to Gordon, the irrational can be understood.

Gordon has found that five interrelated states of mind must be present in order for an individual to move through the creative process and make the breakthroughs that contribute to a final solution. These are:

1. detachment and involvement
2. deferment
3. speculation
4. autonomy
5. hedonic response

Practically, this means that when students are working on a problem, it is necessary to detach them from their present activity and to involve them in a new problem. Help them to defer completing the task by not choosing the easiest answer, and move them on to more complex ideas. After the students have deferred the easy solution, engage them in speculation about new possibilities and new ways

[1]William J. Gordon, *Synectics* (New York:Harper & Row, 1961), p. 6.
[2]*Ibid.*, p. 1.

of looking at the problem. Finally, return to the autonomy of the creative process: allow the students to form a solution, one that incorporates the ideas drawn from the other activities. The hedonic response is a subtle feeling traditionally known as inspiration or intuition. It tells a person that the solution or hypothesis is right. It is not simply being correct. It is the pleasurable feeling that comes from knowing that the problem can be resolved or the idea can be expressed in a uniquely new creative way. It is a completion of the circle that began with detachment.

The goal of Synectics training for teachers is to help them design procedures that will enable them to draw their students into the psychological states necessary for creative activity. These procedures are illustrated in Figure 2. Each phase is distinct, yet they are all connected. You will find a parallel between these psychological states and the phases of the Synectics Model. Through the use of a sequence of metaphoric activities, Synectics draws students into the states of deferment, speculation, autonomy, and innovation.

Metaphoric Activity: The Key to Synectics

The basic activity of the Synectics Model is metaphor. Through metaphoric activity, creativity becomes a conscious process. Metaphors establish a relationship of likeness, the comparison of one object or idea with another object or idea by using one in place of the other. Through these substitutions the creative process occurs, connecting the familiar with the unfamiliar or creating a new idea from two familiar ideas.

Metaphor introduces conceptual distance between the student and the object or subject matter and allows time to think reflectively. During metaphoric activity, students innovate and imagine. The conceptual distance in metaphoric activity creates emotional involvement by providing the student with the freedom and the structure to move into new ways of thinking. For example, by asking students to think of their textbook as an old shoe or as a river, we provide a structure, a

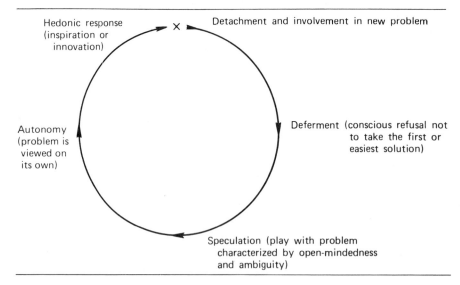

Figure 2. *The Psychological States Necessary for Creative Activity.*

metaphor with which the students can think about something familiar in a new way. Conversely, we can ask students to think about a new topic, say the human body, in an old way. For example, we can ask them to compare it to the transportation system. By doing this, we can make the unfamiliar familiar. Thus, metaphoric activity depends upon and draws upon the students' knowledge. It is a way to help students connect ideas from familiar content with those from new content, or to view familiar content from a new perspective. Synectic strategies using metaphoric activity are designed, then, to provide a support structure through which students can free themselves to develop imagination and insight into everyday activities.

Evocative Questions: Stimuli to Metaphoric Activity

Metaphoric activity is initiated by the teacher asking *evocative questions*. Evocative questions are open-ended queries intended to draw all class members into the creative process. The teacher opens the discussion with evocative questions designed to arouse student interest. Throughout the discussion, the teacher uses evocative questions to help students connect old and new information, to relate abstract ideas to past experience, and to innovate when faced with a problem or an unfamiliar situation. The teacher assists, but does not manipulate, students as they organize and expand their ideas, encouraging the development of detailed analogies. As the class moves through the psychological states of the creative process, the teacher uses evocative questions to enable students achieve conceptual distance. For example, the judicious use of evocative questions helps students decide why they like some metaphors better than others.

Types of Metaphor

Gordon has identified three types of metaphor: direct analogy, personal analogy, and compressed conflict. Each type is employed in the Synectics strategies, but metaphoric activity can be used apart from either strategy to warm up students for creativity. We have called this use of metaphor "stretching exercises."

In the following sections, we describe each type of metaphor. Also, we use stretching exercises to help you to understand each type of analogy and to loosen up and become comfortable and familiar with metaphorical activities. Work through all of the exercises. Don't be concerned if in the first exercise you cannot find the exact word or idea you want to express. Your ability to create metaphors will increase as you work your way through the activities.

Direct Analogy

Direct analogy is a simple comparison of two objects or concepts. The comparison does not have to be identical in all respects. Its function is simply to transpose the conditions of the real topic or problem situation to another situation in order to present a new view of an idea or problem. In order for students to use direct analogy, they need to be taught how to analogize the conditions of the problem into new settings. They must learn how to move from the general to the particular.

Gordon has identified *levels of strain* that separate the comparisons. As in all analogies, the greater the strangeness or originality of an idea, the greater its conceptual distance and the greater its usefulness for fostering creativity. The levels of strain represent the process of the mind as it stretches during metaphorical activity. The levels of strain become apparent during the five psychological states Gordon has identified as part of the creative process: (1) detachment and involvement, (2) deferment, (3) speculation, (4) autonomy, and (5) hedonic response. To illustrate his point, Gordon compares a wheel of a car to other objects as they rotate. These objects move from the general to the particular; the final choice is quite specific:

1. the cutter on a can opener
2. the rotor on a helicopter
3. the orbit of Mars
4. a spinning seed pod
5. a hoop snake

We can impose these levels of strain on Figure 2 in order to show how the mind uses strain to push itself to innovation or inspiration (see Figure 3).

Two points of caution should be offered here about all analogies. First, analogies are highly individual aesthetic responses, so there will be considerable difference among the responses offered. The levels of strain are only guidelines for metaphorical activity. Each example is not *the* answer, but rather one person's answer. Second, the age of the students will affect their skill in using metaphor and the amount of formal discussion about metaphorical skills that can be undertaken. Young children have a more limited experience and tend to offer more general metaphors, whereas older students welcome the opportunity to explore their ideas for a longer period of time and become very particular.

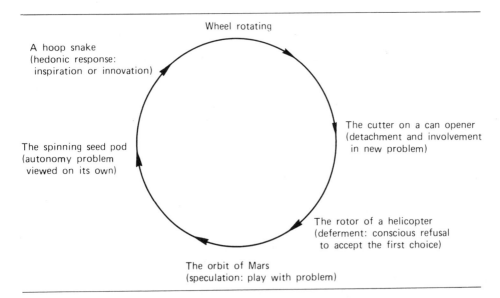

Figure 3. *Example of a Metaphor.*

EXERCISE 1: DIRECT ANALOGY

Moving through the levels of strain with students helps them to stretch their creativity. Before we move on to personal analogy, try to work through each of these levels by comparing an automobile engine to something else. Use the format, "An automobile engine is like a _____ because _____ ."

1. _____ (detachment and involvement in new problem)

2. _____ (deferment: conscious refusal to accept first choice)

3. _____ (speculation: play with problem)

4. _____ (autonomy: problem viewed on its own)

5. _____ (inspiration or innovation)

Another example of a direct analogy might be, "A storm is like a _____ (supply the name of a machine) because _____ ."

A final example of direct analogy would be to think of something from the plant world that is like a wheel. _____

Personal Analogy

Personal analogy requires students to involve themselves through empathetic identification with the ideas or objects to be compared. Students feel that they have become part of the physical elements of the problem. The identification may be with a person, plant, or animal, or with a nonliving thing. For example, students may be instructed, "Be an automobile engine. What do you feel like? Describe how you feel when you are turned on; when your battery goes dead; when you come to a stop light."

In discussing personal analogy, Gordon notes that its application requires extensive loss of self. The greater the conceptual distance created by loss of self, the more likely it is that the analogy is new and that the students have created or innovated. Gordon identifies four levels of involvement in a personal analogy:

1. First-person description of facts: The person recites a list of well-known facts but presents no new way of viewing the object or animal and shows no empathetic involvement. In terms of the car engine, the person might say, "I feel greasy" or, "I feel hot."

2. First-person identification with emotion: The person recites common emotions but does not present new insights. "I feel powerful" (as the car engine).

3. Empathetic identification with a living thing: The student identifies emotionally and kinesthetically with the subject of the analogy. "I feel like my parts are racing around. I'm in a hurry" (as the car engine).

4. Empathetic identification with a nonliving object: This level requires the most commitment. The person sees himself as an inorganic object and tries to explore the problem from a sympathetic point of view. "I feel

exploited. I cannot determine when I start and stop. Someone does that for me" (as the car engine).

The purpose of introducing these levels of personal analogy is not to identify forms of metaphoric activity but to provide guidelines for how well conceptual distance has been established. Gordon believes that the usefulness of analogies is directly proportional to the distance created. The greater the distance, the more likely the student is to come up with new ideas. It is apparent to us, as it will soon be to you, that in generating personal analogies you will frequently overlap or combine these four categories. Each of these levels of metaphoric activity will be clearer after you read some examples and try to create some metaphors for yourself. Distinguishing among the levels is surprisingly easy after you have tried it a few times.

EXERCISE 2: FIRST-PERSON DESCRIPTION OF FACTS

This is the easiest level of metaphoric activity. Compare yourself to a physical object. For example, "How would I look if I were a bulldozer?" "How would I look if I were a flower?" "How would I look if I were a caterpillar?" "How would it feel to be a school?"

Try several of these metaphors, but limit yourself to a physical description: how would you look, how would you move? If you are working with other people, share your ideas:

If I were a _____ , I would look like _____ .

If I were a _____ , I would look like _____ .

If I were a _____ , I would move like _____ .

EXERCISE 3: FIRST-PERSON IDENTIFICATION WITH EMOTION

This level requires more detachment. It poses questions such as "How would I feel if I were a bulldozer? A flower? A caterpillar?" This level also emphasizes empathetic involvement with emotions: "How would it feel to be *love*?" "How would it feel to be *hate*?" "How would it feel to be *ambivalence*?"

Try several of these metaphors, expressing your emotional reaction. Try to detach yourself from physical aspects, and draw on the emotional aspects of an object. Again, if you are working with others, share your ideas.

If I were a _____ , I would feel _____ .

If I were a _____ , I would feel _____ .

If I were a _____ , I would feel _____ .

Now try to connect yourself with feeling an emotion.

If I were _____ , I would feel _____ .

If I were _____ , I would feel _____ .

If I were _____ , I would feel _____ .

EXERCISE 4: EMPATHETIC IDENTIFICATION WITH A LIVING THING

This level combines aspects of the first two levels. The student is able to describe the physical appearance of the living thing as well as to empathize with its emotions. "How would I feel if I were a lonely child?" combines the physical and emotional aspects of the first two levels. Other examples of this level would be: "How would I feel if I were stood up on my first date?" "How would I feel if I got an A on my exam?" As you begin to work with this level, you may find it necessary to work through the first two levels before you can find the right analogy. All forms of metaphoric activity are cumulative and depend on one another in developing sophisticated metaphor. Try an example here and discuss the process if you are working with others.

First-Person Description of Facts:

First-Person Identification With Emotion:

Empathetic Identification With a Living Thing:

EXERCISE 5: EMPATHETIC IDENTIFICATION WITH A NONLIVING THING

The fourth level of personal analogy (Empathetic Identification With a Nonliving Thing) has been best demonstrated to us by the recent craze over the Pet Rock. But it could be used to describe and to help the students understand abstract concepts such as patriotism and liberty. Some other examples of this level of personal analogy are identification with a pencil or a musical instrument. Again, as you begin to work with this level, it may be necessary to work through the first two levels and then combine your results into a final metaphor. Discuss your comparison if you are working in a group.

First-Person Description of Facts:

First-Person Identification With Emotion:

Empathetic Identification With a Nonliving Thing:

The purpose in presenting the different levels of personal analogy is to emphasize the complexity of the analogies that are possible. The more complex the analogy, the farther the students place themselves from the original idea and the greater their opportunity for creativity and originality of thought.

Compressed Conflict

The third type of analogy is compressed conflict, a description of an object or idea consisting of two words that seem to be opposite or contradictory to each other. The purpose of the compressed conflict in fostering creativity is to provide a broad insight into a new subject and to maximize the surprise factor. Compressed conflict is an analytical process requiring students to observe or speculate on an object or idea from different frames of reference. Two examples of compressed conflict are "pretty awful" and "tiredly aggressive."

EXERCISE 6: COMPRESSED CONFLICT

Compressed conflict is a more difficult metaphor than personal or direct analogy because it requires greater conceptual distance. See if you can respond to the questions below. Each develops or describes a compressed conflict.

What machine is a smile and a frown? _____

How is a computer shy and aggressive? _____

What two words that fight each other (or seem to be opposite) can you use to describe the sun? _____

Essential to compressed conflict is the idea of combining paradoxical points of view about the same object or idea; to be able to see the object or idea from two frames of reference is crucial. Again, younger children will enjoy the idea of combining opposites, but their level of strain or internal conflict may not be as great as that of older children. However, don't hesitate to use all three types of metaphor; younger children's freedom with language creates many fascinating phrases and expressions.

Each of the three types of metaphoric activity has its own characteristics. As you spend more time working with metaphors, you will see how the analogies can blend together and how they can remain quite distinct. The next section describes possibilities for incorporating metaphoric activity into classroom strategies.

Before you go on, however, it might be useful to see how well you understand the three types of metaphoric activity. Exercise 7 contains several examples. See if you can identify them.

EXERCISE 7: METAPHOR REVIEW

Label the following examples DA (direct analogy), P (personal analogy), or CC (compressed conflict).

_____ 1. How is a computer shy and aggressive?

_____ 2. An orange is like _____ .

_____ 3. What machine is like a smile and a frown?

_____ 4. Rain is like _____ (supply the name of a machine) because _____ .

_____ 5. Be a cloud. Where are you? What are you doing? How do you feel?

_____ 6. Imagine you are a waterfall. Describe how you feel and think.

How did you do? If you labeled 1 CC, 2 DA, 3 CC, 4 DA, 5 P, and 6 P, you answered them all correctly. If you missed some, perhaps you need to read the section on metaphoric activity again.

The Synectics Model: Two Strategies for Enhancing Creativity

The Synectics Model is built upon the metaphoric mechanisms that we have been describing. The sequence of metaphoric activity is the basis of the phases of the model. There are actually two strategies or models of teaching based on Synectics procedures. One of these (Creating Something New) is designed to make the familiar strange, to help students see old problems, ideas, or products in a new, more creative light. The other strategy (Making the Strange Familiar) is designed to make new, unfamiliar ideas more meaningful; we do this by using familiar analogies. Although both strategies employ the three types of analogy, their objectives, syntax, and principles of reaction are different. We refer to Creating Something New as Strategy One, and Making the Strange Familiar as Strategy Two.

Strategy One tries to help the students see familiar things in unfamiliar ways. It does this by using analogies to create conceptual distance. Except for the final step, in which the students return to the original problem, they do not make simple comparisons. The objective of this strategy may be to develop a new understanding; an empathetic view of a show-off or bully; a new design for a doorway or city; new solutions to social or interpersonal problems, such as a garbage strike or how to stop two students from fighting with each other; or personal problems, such as how to concentrate better when reading. The role of the teacher is to guard against premature analyses and closure. Study the syntax of Strategy One in Figure 4.

Phase One: Description of Present Condition	Phase Two: Direct Analogy	Phase Three: Personal Analogy
Teacher gets students' description of situation or topic as they see it now.	Students suggest direct analogies, select one, and explore (describe) it further.	Students "become" the analogy they selected in Phase Two.
Phase Four: **Compressed Conflict**	**Phase Five:** **Direct Analogy**	**Phase Six:** **Reexamination of the** **Original Task**
Students take their descriptions from Phases Two and Three, suggest several compressed conflicts, and choose one.	Students generate and select another direct analogy, based on the compressed conflict.	Teacher gets students to move back to original task or problem and utilize the last analogy and/or the entire Synectics experience.

Figure 4. *Syntax for Creating Something New.*

As you can see from Figure 5, these phases reflect Gordon's view of the psychological state that is conducive to metaphor.

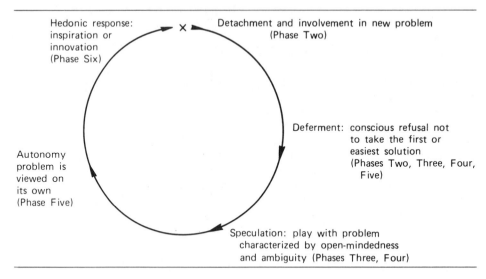

Figure 5. *The Ring of Creativity.*

The role of the teacher in this strategy is complex. The teacher needs to openly display a use of the nonrational and to encourage the students to indulge in fancy, irrelevance, fantasy, symbolism, and other nonrational states of mind that are necessary in order for them to break out of conventional ways of thinking. Teachers must be willing to accept the bizarre and unusual; students must be made to feel that their responses are being accepted without judgment. The more difficult the problem, the more the teacher must accept far-fetched analogies in order to help students break away from conventional ideas and develop fresh perspectives on problems.

The objective of Strategy Two, Making the Strange Familiar, is to increase the students' understanding and internalization of substantially new or difficult material. The metaphoric mechanism in this analogy is used for *analysis*, not for creating conceptual distance, as in Strategy One. For instance, the teacher might present the concept of culture to her class. Using more familiar analogies (such as a stove or a house), the students begin to define the characteristics that are present and those that are lacking in the concept. The strategy is decidedly analytical, and convergent. The students constantly alternate between defining the characteristics of the more familiar subject and comparing these to the characteristics of the unfamiliar topic.

In Phase One of this strategy, the explanation of the new topic, the students are provided with information. In Phase Two the teacher, or the students, suggests a direct analogy. Phase Three involves "being the familiar" (personalizing the direct analogy). In Phase Four, students make connections between the analogy and the substantive material and then explain the connections. That is, they identify and explain the points of similarity. In Phase Five, the students examine the differences between analogies. As a measure of their acquisition of the new information, the students can suggest and analyze their own familiar analogies for Phases Six and Seven. Study the syntax of Strategy Two in Figure 6.

Phase One: Substantive Input	Phase Two: Direct Analogy	Phase Three: Personal Analogy
Teacher provides information on new topic.	Teacher suggests direct analogy and asks students to describe the analogy.	Teacher gets students to "become" the direct analogy.
Phase Four: **Comparing Analogies**	**Phase Five:** **Explaining Differences**	**Phase Six:** **Exploration**
Students identify and explain the points of similarity between the new material and the direct analogy.	Students explain where the analogy doesn't fit.	Students re-explore the original topic on its own terms.
	Phase Seven: **Generating Analogy**	
	Students provide their own direct analogy and explore the similarities and differences.	

Figure 6. *Syntax for Making the Strange Familiar.*

The major difference between the two strategies lies in their use of analogy. In Strategy One, the students move through a series of analogies without logical constraints, tying them to an original point of reference; conceptual distance is increased, and imagination is free to wander. In Strategy Two, the students try to connect two ideas and to identify the connections as they move through the analogies. Which strategy you use depends on your objectives. Are you trying to help students create something new or explore the unfamiliar?

Using Synectics in the Curriculum

Synectics is a strategy designed to increase the creativity of individuals and groups. Sharing the Synectics experience can help build a feeling of community among students. Students learn about their fellow classmates as they watch them react to an idea or problem. Thoughts are valued for their potential contribution to the group process. Synectics procedures help create a community of equals in which simply having a thought is the sole basis for status. This norm and that of playfulness quickly give support to even the most timid participant.

Synectics procedures may be used with students in all areas of the curriculum, the sciences as well as the arts. The Synectics procedures can be used both in teacher-student discussion in the classroom and in teacher-made materials for the students. The products or vehicles of Synectics activity need not always be written. They can be oral, or they can take the form of role plays, paintings and graphics, or simply changes in behavior. When using Synectics to look at social or behavior problems, you may wish to notice situational behavior changes before and after Synectics activity. It is also interesting to select modes of expression that contrast with the original topic, such as having students paint a picture of prejudice or discrimination. The concept is abstract, but the mode of expression is concrete.

Synectics is a model designed to increase creativity. The creative process and its accompanying emotional states are useful in many types of learning situations and in almost all curriculum areas. Some possible uses are discussed in the following paragraphs.

Creative Writing. Strategy One of the Synectics Model is an excellent instructional strategy for developing creative writing abilities. Writing, either expository writing about a particular concept (such as friendship) or more personalized writing (regarding an emotion or an experience), is an area of the language arts program for which Synectics has great potential. Through Synectics procedures, the students can develop a highly creative style of expression. The metaphoric activity stimulates their imagination and helps them record their thoughts and feelings.

Exploring Social Problems. Strategy One is an excellent teaching strategy for exploring social and disciplinary problems. The metaphor creates a distance, so the confrontation does not include a threat to the learner. The distance permits discussion and self-examination. The personal analogy phase is critical for developing insight.

Problem Solving. Problem solving that is concerned with social issues, interpersonal relations, or intrapersonal problems is amenable to Synectics. The objective of Strategy Two is to break set, conceptualizing the problem in a new way in order to suggest fresh approaches to it. An example of a social issue would be how to better relations between the police and the community. Reducing family spending is an example of an interpersonal relations problem. Intrapersonal problems might include how to stop fighting with a friend, how to do math lessons, how to feel better about wearing glasses, and how to stop making fun of people.

Creating a Design or Product. Synectics can also be used to create a product or design. The product is something tangible, such as a painting, a building, or a bookshelf, whereas the design is a plan, such as an idea for a party or new means of transportation. Eventually, designs or plans become real, but for the purposes of this model they remain as sketches or outlines.

Broadening Our Perspective of a Concept. Abstract ideas such as culture, prejudice, and economy are difficult to internalize because we cannot see them in the same way we can see a table or building, yet we frequently use them in our language. Synectics is a good way to make a "familiar" idea "strange" and thereby obtain another perspective on it.

Summary

Synectics is a process for promoting creativity. Building upon unconventional assumptions about creativity, William Gordon developed procedures for fostering creativity through a group process. The basic activity of Synectics is metaphoric thinking. There are three types of metaphor: direct analogy, personal analogy, and compressed conflict. Two models of teaching have been developed on the basis of Synectics procedures: Creating Something New and Making the Strange Familiar. They are very similar, except that the former uses metaphor to encourage divergent thinking and the indulgence of fancy, whereas the latter is convergent, analytic, and logical, in that students compare aspects of the new material to the more familiar analogy.

SUMMARY CHART: SYNECTICS MODEL

Syntax (Strategy One: Creating Something New)

Phase One: Description of Present Condition
Teacher gets students' description of situation or topic as they see it now.

Phase Two: Direct Analogy
Students suggest direct analogies, select one, and explore (describe) it further.

Phase Three: Personal Analogy
Students "become" the analogy they selected in Phase Two.

Phase Four: Compressed Conflict
Students take their descriptions from Phases Two and Three, suggest several compressed conflicts, and choose one.

Phase Five: Direct Analogy
Students generate and select another direct analogy, based on the compressed conflict.

Phase Six: Reexamination of the Original Task
Teacher gets students to move back to original task or problem and utilize the last analogy and/or the entire synectics experience.

Syntax (Strategy Two: Making the Strange Familiar)

Phase One: Substantive Input
Teacher provides information on new topic.

Phase Two: Direct Analogy
Teacher suggests direct analogy and asks students to describe the analogy.

Phase Three: Personal Analogy
Teacher gets students to "become" the direct analogy.

Phase Four: Comparing Analogies
Students identify and explain the points of similarity between the new material and the direct analogy.

Phase Five: Explaining Differences
Students explain where the analogy doesn't fit.

Phase Six: Exploration
Students re-explore the original topic on its own terms.

Phase Seven: Generating Analogy
Students can provide their own direct analogy and explore the similarities and differences.

Principles of Reaction

The teacher accepts all student responses and insures that students feel no external judgment on their creative expression. However, by the choice of evocative questions, the teacher can clarify their expression and stimulate creative thinking. The teacher can also act as exemplar of the model, thereby demonstrating the norms of the play of fancy. In Strategy One, the teacher guards against premature analysis and reflects the students' problem-solving behavior to them. That is, the teacher clarifies and summarizes the progress of the learning activity.

Social System

The social system for the synectics model is moderately structured. The teacher initiates and guides the students through the metaphorical problem solving. The discussions are open-ended; norms of intellectual freedom and equality prevail. The rewards for the students are the internal satisfaction and pleasure that result from the learning experience.

Support System

The support system for this model consists of teacher familiarity with Synectics procedures, a comfortable environment, and a laboratory or other appropriate resources if scientific or design problems are being considered.

THEORY IN PRACTICE

No amount of description can convey a sense of a model of teaching as well as an example of the model in practice. In fact, reading too much theory before gaining a rough "image" of the practice can be confusing and, for some people, frustrating and discouraging. So we encourage you, at this point of your study of the Synectics Model, to read the following abbreviated transcript of an actual classroom session. We suggest that you first read only the teacher-student dialogue and then go back to note the annotations. Remember, the goal at this point in your training is to gain a sense of the model—its flow and feeling—not to master the techniques of implementation.

In this lesson, the teacher uses Strategy One (Creating Something New) to talk about a child who is the class behavior problem. The metaphoric activity builds through the phases and concludes with a sample of student writing from the exercise. The teacher combines both oral and written modes of expression in the lesson.

Notice how the teacher asks key questions that move the students through the phases. How does the teacher serve as an exemplar? How does the teacher encourage playfulness? Can you identify the psychological stages of the creative process as they occur? As the children work through the exercise, you may want to make notes about the metaphors that *you* would use. This will help you to empathize with the process that the students are undergoing.

T: TODAY WE ARE GOING TO TALK AND WRITE ABOUT A LITTLE BOY WHO IS ALWAYS GETTING INTO TROUBLE. HE IS A PEST, AND ALL THE TEACHERS THINK HE IS BAD. TAKE A FEW MINUTES AND WRITE ABOUT SOME OF THE THINGS THAT HE DOES.

Phase One: Describing the Present Condition
Teacher asks for a description of the boy. Students describe the boy.

S: HE HITS THE OTHER KIDS.

S: HE ALWAYS RUNS AROUND THE ROOM.

S: HE THROWS SPITBALLS.

S: HE WON'T LISTEN TO ME WHEN I TALK TO HIM.

T: WHAT ELSE DID YOU SAY ABOUT HIM?

S: HE OPENS THE WINDOW AND HE'S NOT SUPPOSED TO.

S: HE JUMPS AROUND A LOT. HE MAKES A LOT OF NOISE.

S: HE IS REALLY SPOILED.

S: HE'S A TROUBLEMAKER. HE'S ALWAYS STEALING THINGS FROM OTHER KIDS.

T: TODAY, WE ARE GOING TO SEE IF WE CAN MAKE SOME COMPARISONS SO THAT WE CAN LEARN MORE ABOUT THIS PERSON. COULD YOU THINK OF SOMETHING THAT YOU COULD COMPARE HIM TO—SOMETHING THAT ISN'T ALIVE. CAN ANYBODY THINK OF SOMETHING?

Phase Two: Direct Analogy

Teacher asks for a direct analogy. He also specifies the nature of the analogy—an inorganic comparison—in order to assure getting one of some distance.

Student suggests a direct analogy.

S: HE IS LIKE A HURRICANE.

T: ANYBODY ELSE?

S: A TORNADO.

T: OKAY. WELL, LET'S DEAL WITH A HURRICANE AND A TORNADO. WHAT ARE THEY LIKE?

Teacher moves students to simply explore the analogy they selected.

Students describe the direct analogy.

S: THEY MOVE ALL AROUND AND THEY SWEEP THINGS UP WITH THEM AND THEY PUSH THINGS BECAUSE THEY'RE STRONG AND FORCEFUL.

S: YOU CAN'T PREDICT THEM, YOU KNOW—THEY JUST POP DOWN IN THE MIDDLE AND THEN THEY'RE UP AGAIN.

S: THEY DESTROY EVERYTHING IN THEIR PATH.

T: WHAT ELSE?

S: THEY'RE NOISY, TOO. YOU CAN'T MISS THEM. THEY JUST COME ALONG AND THEY ARE SELF-CENTERED.

T: LET'S SEE NOW IF YOU CAN "BE" THAT HURRICANE OR TORNADO. HOW DOES IT FEEL TO BE THAT HURRICANE OR TORNADO? BE THE THING.

Phase Three: Personal Analogy

Students "become" the thing.

S: POWERFUL.

S: TWISTED.

T: YOU FEEL TWISTED INSIDE.

S: I FEEL MEAN INSIDE. I AM ALWAYS GRABBING THINGS. I NEVER STAY AT ONE THING AT ONE TIME. I AM ALWAYS MOVING ON TO THE NEXT THING. I AM VERY INVOLVED IN WHAT I AM DOING.

S: I AM TIRED BECAUSE YOU HAVE TO MOVE, YOU KNOW. YOU CAN'T EVER STOP.

S: I KNOW THAT PEOPLE DON'T LIKE ME. THEY ARE AFRAID OF ME, BUT I TRY NOT TO CARE.

T: PICK TWO WORDS THAT YOU USED IN YOUR COMPARISON THAT SEEM TO FIGHT EACH OTHER, THAT ARE OPPOSITES OF EACH OTHER.

S: POWERFUL AND TWISTED.

S: STRONG AND DESTRUCTIVE.

S: TIRED AND TWISTED.

S: YOU HAVE SUGGESTED THREE PAIRS, POWERFUL AND TWISTED, STRONG AND DESTRUCTIVE, TIRED AND TWISTED. WHICH PAIR SHALL WE USE?

S: I THINK TIRED AND TWISTED.

S: YES, THAT'S GOOD.

T: IS IT ALL RIGHT WITH EVERYONE? LET'S USE THEM, THE WORDS TIRED AND TWISTED. CAN YOU THINK OF AN ANALOGY THAT WOULD FIT THESE WORDS? ANOTHER PERSON OR THING?

S: SOME KIND OF A MACHINE, YOU KNOW—LIKE A DRILL, A DRILL THAT CONSTRUCTION WORKERS USE.

T: HOW DO THE WORDS TIRED AND TWISTED FIT THE DRILL?

S: I WOULD BE TWISTING SO LONG AND I WOULD BE DOING IT SO OFTEN THAT I WOULD EVENTUALLY GET TIRED OF DOING IT, AND I WOULD WANT TO STOP FOR A WHILE AND JUST RELAX.

S: IT'S LIKE YOU HAVE NO CONTROL OVER YOURSELF. SOMEONE ELSE IS RUNNING YOU. YOU GET TIRED. YOU DON'T HAVE ANY CHOICE ABOUT TWISTING AND TURNING; YOU HAVE TO KEEP GOING.

S: I GET SO TIRED. I GUESS I JUST REALLY DON'T WANT TO DO THIS TWISTING.

S: I JUST WANT TO TAKE A REST, AND IF I WERE THE DRILL, THEN I'D SAY TO MYSELF, "IT'S JUST WHAT I WANT TO DO; I'M TIRED AND I WANT TO TAKE A REST."

S: THE ONLY WAY TO TAKE A REST IS TO WEAR YOURSELF OUT. YOU CAN'T STOP; YOU HAVE TO BREAK DOWN TO STOP.

S: I WANT SOMEONE TO STOP ME—TO TURN ME OFF.

T: OK, WHAT WOULD BE ALIKE IN TERMS OF THIS DRILL AND THIS BOY?

S: THEY WOULD MAKE A LOT OF NOISE.

S: HE HAS NO CONTROL OVER HIMSELF.

S: AND HE DIGS INTO THINGS AND UPSETS THINGS ALL THE TIME.

T: ANYTHING ELSE ABOUT THE MACHINE—THIS PARTICULAR DRILL MACHINE?

S: IT JUST DOES THE SAME THINGS OVER AND OVER AGAIN.

S: IT'S ANNOYING PEOPLE. WHEN PEOPLE WALK BY THIS KIND OF MACHINE, I GUESS THEY GET VERY ANNOYED BECAUSE IT'S NOISY AND IT'S

Phase Four: Compressed Conflict
Teacher asks for compressed conflicts as an outgrowth of the personal anology.

Students suggest various compressed conflicts.

Phase Five: New Direct Analogy
The compressed conflict is not explored in itself, but serves as the basis for the new direct analogy.

Teacher asks students to force-fit the compressed conflict into the new direct analogy.

Teacher moves to obtain more information about the new analogy.

VERY IRRITATING—PEOPLE GET VERY IRRI-
TATED BY IT.

S: THEY TURN AWAY. THEY DON'T WANT TO LISTEN.
THEY COVER THEIR EARS.

S: THE BOY COULD THINK AND COULD CHANGE
HIMSELF IF HE WANTED TO, NOT LIKE THE
DRILL.

S: A DRILL YOU TURN ON AND TURN OFF, AND A
BOY MIGHT NEED HELP DOING THAT BUT
EVENTUALLY HE COULD LEARN TO DO IT BY
HIMSELF.

T: THAT WAS ALL VERY INTERESTING. NOW, I'LL
TELL YOU WHAT I'D LIKE YOU TO DO. I'D LIKE
YOU TO TAKE THREE MINUTES AND AGAIN
WRITE SOMETHING ABOUT THIS BOY. USE ALL
THE IDEAS YOU RECEIVED FROM THE COM-
PARISONS WE MADE TOGETHER. YOU COULD
WRITE ABOUT SOMETHING THAT YOU WANT
SOMEONE ELSE TO READ SO THAT THEY'LL
UNDERSTAND THIS BOY AND WHAT HE IS ALL
ABOUT. YOU HAVE TO REMEMBER THAT THEY
DON'T KNOW THIS BOY AND YOU HAVE TO GIVE
THIS PERSON A PICTURE OF THE BOY THROUGH
YOUR WRITING. OK, WRITE A PARAGRAPH ABOUT
THIS BOY.

Phase Six: Reexamination of the Original Task
Teacher asks the students to reexamine the
original task, using comparisons to elicit new
dimensions of the characterization. How is
the original problem explored now?

New dimensions of original problem.

Samples of Student Writing

1. Tired, weary, I must keep going. Perhaps someone will help me focus my energies. Why do people turn away? I'll show them! I'll keep busting up their party.

2. This boy is all twisted inside; he is full of energy, but like a tornado he always uses it by destroying things. He does this continually, hardly ever stopping to catch his breath. He feels tired sometimes, and it is then that he slows down. He can control his behavior, but a tornado cannot.

3. They think I'm bad and that I misbehave, but I don't really want to. I just don't have any other way to get people's attention and make them notice me. I know I annoy them sometimes, but at least they know I'm around and alive. If my teacher would just look at me and try to understand my problems; but no, he's always yelling and screaming and calling me a nuisance. So that's what I'll be like.

4. Our boy has almost no control over his own actions. It's as if he were completely dominated by some outside influence; like a hurricane or tornado, he's twisting and turning, destroying every-thing in his path. The only way to stop is to burn himself up. When his energy has been used up, he finally stops.

TAKING \THEORY INTO ACTION

In this section, we are going to "walk through" a Synectics lesson. We will begin with some stretching exercises, then move through a lesson, and, finally, try to evaluate the success of the metaphoric activity. Again, we strongly urge you to work with other people as you complete the activities in this reading. Sharing your ideas will facilitate the group dynamics of the Synectics process and contribute to a playful mood, which can greatly expand individual creativity. If you work alone, concentrate on moving rapidly through the exercises. There is no "right" answer to any of the questions, so do not ponder any of your responses. Rely on your feelings to move you along.

In the first exercise we simply want you to feel what it's like to move away from the original problem or task, focus on something entirely different, and then return to the original problem with a fresh perspective. We do not go through all the types of metaphor, or phases of activity, in this exercise.

EXERCISE 1: CREATING SOMETHING NEW

Imagine you are a foreign-language teacher. You are trying to get your students to speak the new language, but they are inhibited and reluctant to converse out loud. How would you go about getting them to communicate to you and to each other in the new language? Jot down a few suggestions in the space below. They do not have to be detailed; a few sketchy thoughts will do.

Look at your ideas. Are any of them particularly new? Try changing your focus. In the space below, write down a few thoughts on learning to drive your car. How did you feel? What was it like? How did you go about it? What steps were involved? Generate as much description of this event as you can.

Now look over your comments on learning to drive, and then refocus on the question of getting students to speak a foreign language. Can you think about the original problem differently? Do you have any new approaches? Try writing out a few statements about your plans for this problem.

Metaphors should force you to see familiar situations in a new context. Did the metaphor of learning to drive enhance your perceptions of the original problem and at the same time increase your emotional involvement by immersing you in the situation of driving a car? If you are working with a group, you may want to pause here and discuss your different approaches to the idea. By describing the familiar analogy and then making the comparison, you put unfamiliar subject matter into a familiar language, so that it can be intellectually clarified, organized, and internalized.

This exercise was based on Strategy One (Creating Something New). If you had trouble with this exercise, felt constrained by its artificiality, or were unable to loosen up enough, you were probably not warmed up enough. Warm-up is essential to Synectics procedures; it is the time for detachment and playfulness. Warming up with stretching exercises sets the stage for the creative activity.

Stretching Exercises: Warm-Ups for Metaphoric Activity

In this section, we present some stretching exercises to help you loosen up and expand your creative consciousness. Stretching exercises provide experience with the three types of metaphoric activity, but they are *not* related to any *particular* problem situation nor do they follow a sequence of phases. As you introduce Synectics to your students, you will want to spend several days incorporating stretching exercises into your lessons so that the students become familiar with metaphoric activity, comfortable with playing with language, and receptive to the model.

Direct analogy is a simple comparison of two objects or concepts. It includes, though it is not necessarily identical in all respects to, the conditions of the real problem situation. The direct analogy transposes the original condition to another situation. In guiding students' work with direct analogy, a teacher must complete three steps:

Step 1. Explore the meaning of comparison with students. To do this, ask yourself what comparison is and how it works.

Step 2. Define direct analogy for your students: "A direct analogy is a way of making connections and comparisons between ideas, people, things, or problems."

Step 3. Work some examples with students.

EXERCISE 2

Compare a plant and a schoolroom. After you generate a comparison, or analogy, you should follow up with a series of questions that elicits a rich description of the analogy. Some questions can be general and open-ended: "What does it look like?" "Describe the plant." Other questions can place the plant in a particular situation: "What is the plant like after a rain?" "What is its life cycle?" These situational questions generally elicit descriptions with greater conceptual distance.

If you like this exercise, try to continue to stretch your creativity. In the next exercise, strive for greater strain or conceptual distance.

EXERCISE 3

A sunny day is like what machine?
What does this machine do?
How big is it?
Describe all the parts of the machine.
Describe all the functions of the machine.
What else do you know about this machine?

EXERCISE 4

The following sentences condense the steps in the two previous exercises. Complete each sentence, stretching your creative powers to make strong, direct analogies.

A house is like _____ because

A teacher is like a blender because

A ghetto is like a human being because

A schoolroom is like what nonliving object?

How is a cloud like a bear?

Your birthday is like

EXERCISE 5

Notice that there are several grammatical variations for direct analogy stretching exercises. In Exercise 1, one analogy was selected and a series of follow-up questions attempted to elicit a rich description of it. Exercise 5 presents direct analogy items that are compressed into one sentence. Choose one of the items from Exercise 4 and write a direct analogy stretching exercise modeled on Exercise 2 or 3. Try this out with your colleagues or your class.

What happened when you tried out your analogy? Were there any problems? List your difficulties below.

Personal analogy is individual identification with a person, plant, animal, or non-living thing for the purpose of comparison. The teacher's emphasis is on empathetic involvement by the students. The teacher should complete two steps in working with this form of analogy:

Step 1. Explain personal analogy to the students.

Step 2. Work through personal analogies with the students. Get them to feel that they are what they are describing. Help them to imagine how they would look, what they would do, and how they would feel if they were the thing being described.

EXERCISE 6

Be a piece of celery. How do you feel?

You are a hurricane blowing in from the ocean. What do you look like? What are you doing? How do you feel? How do you feel when you are seeded by an airplane? What do you dislike the most?

You are nice green, cool grass. That is the way you look. How do you feel? How do you feel when someone steps on you? What are three wishes you have?

You are a chair in someone's home. Describe yourself in every way you can.

You are a vacuum cleaner. What can you tell us about yourself?

Be a horse. Tell us everything about yourself that you can.

Be an automobile. How are you different from all other cars?

As you worked through these exercises, were you able to sense a greater willingness on your part to play with ideas, to strain your imagination when making connections? This is the goal of the stretching exercises. As the teacher in the model, you will want to help your students feel this same sense of playfulness and willingness to strain their imaginations.

EXERCISE 7

Choose *one* of the items from the list of personal analyses in Exercise 6 and write how you would teach the personal analogy to your colleagues or class. Follow the procedures from the previous exercises. As with direct analogies, different types of questions can be framed to produce rich descriptions of the personal analogy.

Did you have any problems? If so, list them below.

A compressed conflict is a description consisting of two words that seem to be opposite or contradictory to each other yet can be used to describe an object, person, place, or situation. Compressed conflicts are excellent aids for developing insight, because the contradiction provides dimensions not easily described in other activities. The teacher must complete two steps in working with compressed conflicts:

Step 1. Explain compressed conflict to students.

Step 2. Work some examples. For instance, the first question below asks you to compare a funny and a sad clown. Work through each part of the exercise, and then form a metaphor that compresses the two characteristics.

EXERCISE 8

A clown is funny and sad. On the one hand, a clown is funny because

On the other hand, a clown is sad because

What phrase could describe a funny and a sad clown?

You have written two paragraphs about the shy, withdrawn person, one at the beginning of the exercise (during Phase One) and one at the end (during Phase Six). Compare and contrast these two paragraphs. What do you see as the major differences between the two? If you have gone through all the phases of this exercise, your last paragraph should contain more insight regarding the person and many more dimensions of his personality and/or behavior. Did you experience a willingness to be playful? Could you feel yourself moving through the psychological process that Gordon has described? If you worked as a group, how do you feel that group dynamics contributed to your working of the strategy?

Assessing the Level of Metaphoric Activity

One way of evaluating Synectics activities is to assess the quality of metaphor in order to measure how creative your students' ideas have become. The quality of metaphoric activity or creative development can be determined by the level of involvement that is demonstrated by the students. Gordon has identified a different means of assessing the level of involvement for each type of metaphor. These means consist of guidelines for teachers to use in evaluating the level of strain and the involvement and conceptual distance achieved by the class. We are including these guidelines to help you better understand the metaphorical way of thinking, the quality of metaphor, and the effect of the creative process. Each of the assessment guidelines is concerned with level of involvement. By this, we mean how much conceptual distance was achieved by the students and how much originality or strain went into their final metaphors.

Direct Analogy

Direct analogy, the metaphorical comparison of two objects or concepts, can be very close or very distant. Distance is the important criterion for measuring the creativeness of the analogy. Distance is similar to level of strain. It is also related to the psychological stages of creativity that we have discussed throughout this component. Living things are organic and nonliving things are inorganic. The level of strain is higher if the comparison is between one organic topic and one inorganic topic than if the topics are both organic or both inorganic. We consider it to be higher because the conceptual distance is greater.

EXERCISE 12

The table below lists several analogies. Categorize these as to whether the comparison is between organic and organic (two living things), inorganic and inorganic (two nonliving things), or organic and inorganic (a living thing and a nonliving thing). Which metaphors do you like best? If you are working with a group, you may want to discuss any differences of opinion. After completing the sample items (1-13), list your direct analogies from the sample lesson just completed and categorize them.

Direct Analogies	Inorganic-Inorganic	Organic-Inorganic	Organic-Organic
1. Schoolroom/plant			
2. Sunny day/machine			
3. Orange/living thing			
4. Storm/machine			
5. Storm/plant			
6. House/birthday			
7. Lion/cloud			
8. Head/wind			
9. Laugh/song			
10. Sun/machine			
11. Living thing/bulldozer			
12. Pencil/snow			
13. Birthday/book			
14.			
15.			
16.			
17.			
18.			

The act of analyzing metaphorical strain is a personal and aesthetic judgment. Consequently, there is no real right answer to the problem of identifying the level of strain. Consensus is not necessarily the desired judgment with a class. It would be better and more productive for later work on creativity to encourage students to explain and analyze their own views of creativity.

Personal Analogy

Personal analogies are assessed in terms of student identification with a person, animal, plant, or nonliving thing. In creating personal analogies, students should experience two kinds of identification: *kinesthetic involvement* and *emotional involvement*. Kinesthetic involvement means the person can get inside the living or nonliving thing and show an understanding of its movement and actions. For example, in describing a dog the student might say, "When I'm hungry, I go all over the house with my nose down, sniffing." There is a conscious loss of self here, expressed in the way a dog actually moves.

Emotional identification refers to a conscious loss of self as the student identifies with the feelings and understanding expressed through the analogy. In describing a hurricane as a personal analogy, the student might say, "Everyone is afraid of me because I am dark and look frightening, but I am so tired of twisting and turning and being alone." The conscious loss of self here is expressed in the identification of the feelings of the hurricane.

EXERCISE 13

In Exercise 11 you wrote two paragraphs about the shy, withdrawn person. If you went through all of the phases in this exercise, your last paragraph should have contained deeper insights regarding the person. List some of your analogies below, and decide if they featured kinesthetic or emotional involvement. Discuss your decisions with your group, and compare your judgments.

Personal Analogy	Kinesthetic Involvement (loss of self through description of movement)	Emotional Involvement (loss of self through identification of feelings)
1.		
2.		
3.		
4.		

Compressed Conflict

The simpler form of a compressed conflict is a two-word contradiction—that is, the two words are opposites of each other. The more advanced form is a phrase that contains the contradiction. "Beautiful/repulsive" is an example of the simple form. "Beautiful repulsive" is an example of the advanced form, which is also the more poetic form. Compressed conflict tries to maximize surprises, and thereby reflects its high level of mental strain.

EXERCISE 14

Reread your work in Exercise 11. Select the compressed conflicts from your writing and note them below, along with the words or phrases that were compressed. Were you able to compress ideas while maintaining distance? Did you maintain a high level of strain? Discuss your evaluation with your peers.

Compressed Conflict	Words or Phrases Compressed
1.	
2.	
3.	
4.	

Each of these three levels of involvement will become clearer with more practice. We will offer you other opportunities to use these levels for evaluation in the other components.

Next Steps

Component I (Description and Understanding) introduces you to the basic ideas of Synectics and gives you some experience with Synectics procedures. Component II contains a demonstration of the actual Synectics lesson. Component III offers guidelines and helps you prepare Synectics work for your class. Either Component II or III would be appropriate next, depending on your needs as you perceive them now. If at any point in the next two components you feel frustrated and unsure of the direction of your work, you may want to return to this component to compare your practice with the theory.

THEORY CHECKUP FOR THE SYNECTICS MODEL

1. Which of the following statements agree with Gordon's view of creativity?

   a. Creativity cannot be described.
   b. Individual and group creativity have similar characteristics.
   c. Creativity in the arts is different from invention or hypothesis formation.
   d. All creativity is characterized by a similar process.
   e. Creativity can be fostered in students.

2. Circle the phrase that best defines a direct analogy.

   a. subjective identification with an object
   b. two-word descriptions that fight each other
   c. a noun
   d. a simple comparison of two objects or concepts

3. Gordon describes three types of activity—direct analogy, personal analogy, and compressed conflict. A term that refers to all three types is:

   a. creativity.
   b. emotional conflict.
   c. metaphoric activity.
   d. problem solving.

4. Circle the phrase that best defines a personal analogy.

   a. emotional identification with an object
   b. two-word definitions that contrast with one another
   c. a verb
   d. a simple comparison of two objects or concepts

5. The Synectics Model would *not* be directly appropriate to which of the following educational objectives?

   a. social problem solving
   b. acquiring factual information
   c. empathy
   d. creativity

6. Stretching exercises are intended to:

   a. narrow options of participants.
   b. increase creative potential.
   c. summarize Synectics activity.
   d. promote compressed conflict.

7. List the phases of the Synectics Model.

8. The Senior Class of P.S. 109 is trying to decide what to give the school as a class gift. Would Synectics be applicable to their dilemma?

    a. yes
    b. no

9. Gordon makes several assumptions about the nature of creativity, some of which are shared by other students of creativity. Which one of the following is *not* one of his beliefs?

    a. Creativity is enhanced by consciousness of the creative process. Also, creativity can be described and trained directly.
    b. "Emotions" and irrational processes are the keys to the creative process.
    c. The creative process is similar in all fields. It is not content-specific, although expectations enhance it.
    d. The process of creating individually is the same as in a group. In fact, the group can enhance creativity by generating many ideas and supporting the play of fancy.

10. Peter Peade, a law student, had a dream one evening. In the dream, he overheard a group of wild elephants talking to one another in a language that sounded very much like French. In their discussions, the wild elephants were planning to sneak into Peter's apartment and steal all of the notes for the Bar exam that Peter had collected during his three years of law school. Which of Gordon's assumptions about creativity is illustrated in Peter's dream?

    a. Fear and anxiety are part of the creative process.
    b. When we are creative, we are half-asleep.
    c. Emotional distance.
    d. Creativity involves the irrational.

11. The criterion for assessing the creativity in a metaphor is

    a. compressed conflict.
    b. conceptual distance.
    c. stretching exercises.
    d. kinetic energy.

12. Before going through a Synectics lesson, Joyce believed that people who bullied other people were arrogant and conceited. After working with metaphoric activity, Joyce saw bullies as frightened, lonely people who really wanted to be liked by others. Which of the following best describes the type of experience?

    a. personal growth
    b. tolerance
    c. compressed conflict
    d. stretching exercises

Key to Theory Checkup

1. b, d, e	7. Phase One: Description of the Topic	8. yes
2. d	Phase Two: Direct Analogy	9. b
3. c	Phase Three: Personal Analogy	10. d
4. a	Phase Four: Compressed Conflict	11. b
5. c	Phase Five: New Direct Analogy	12. a
6. b	Phase Six: Reexamination of the Original Task	

Component II

VIEWING
THE MODEL

One of the purposes of Component II is to provide examples of actual sessions in which the Synectics Model is the strategy being used. Reading the demonstration transcript that follows, hearing a tape of a teacher and students, or viewing a video-tape of class activity are alternate means of illustrating the "model in action."

As you study any of these alternatives, you will be introduced to the Teaching Analysis Guide for analyzing the model. This same Guide will also be used in Component III to analyze the peer teaching and microteaching lessons. We want you to become familiar with the Guide now, however, as it will sharpen your perception of the demonstration lesson.

The two activities in this component are (1) reading the Teaching Analysis Guide and (2) viewing (reading) the lesson. Before going on to them, you may wish to reread the material in the Introduction to this book that discusses the purposes and philosophy of the Teaching Analysis Guide.

Analyzing the Teaching: Activity 1

Read through the items in the Teaching Analysis Guide that follows. Identify the items you do not understand. Discuss any difficulties you may have with your instructor or with a peer.

TEACHING ANALYSIS GUIDE FOR THE SYNECTICS MODEL (CREATING SOMETHING NEW)

This Guide is designed to help you analyze the process of teaching as you practice Synectics. The analysis focuses on aspects of teaching that are important to the syntax of the model, the teacher's role, and specific teaching skills.

The Guide consists of a series of questions and phrases. As you observe a practice session (whether peer teaching or microteaching), analyze the teaching using the rating scale that appears opposite each question and statement. The scale uses the following items:

Thoroughly. This item signifies that the teacher engaged in the behavior to the point where students were responding comfortably and fluently. Appropriateness varies from situation to situation.

Partially. This item signifies that the teacher engaged in appropriate behavior, but not as thoroughly as possible. There is some doubt about whether the students are responding fully.

Missing. The teacher did not engage in the behavior; there appears to be a loss in student response or probably will be one.

Not Needed. The teacher did not explicitly manifest the behavior, but there is no loss. Either the behavior was included in others or the students began to respond appropriately without being led to.

For each question or statement in the Guide, circle the term that best describes the teacher's behavior.

Phase One: Description

1. Did the teacher elicit ideas from students about the topic?	Thoroughly	Partially	Missing	Not Needed

Phase Two: Direct Analogy

2. Did the teacher define a direct analogy?	Thoroughly	Partially	Missing	Not Needed
3. Did the teacher specify the type of analogy, such as nonliving or machine?	Thoroughly	Partially	Missing	Not Needed
4. Did the teacher elicit analogies?	Thoroughly	Partially	Missing	Not Needed
5. Did the category of analogy appropriately contrast the topic? (For example, if the topic was a living thing, such as a shy child, was the category of analogies nonliving things, such as a machine?)	Thoroughly	Partially	Missing	Not Needed
6. Did the teacher elicit several analogies?	Thoroughly	Partially	Missing	Not Needed
7. If necessary, did the teacher ask students to clarify their suggested analogies?	Thoroughly	Partially	Missing	Not Needed

63

TEACHING ANALYSIS GUIDE FOR THE SYNECTICS MODEL (CREATING SOMETHING NEW)

8. Did the students select one analogy to work with?	Thoroughly	Partially	Missing	Not Needed
9. Was the analogy familiar to all the students?	Thoroughly	Partially	Missing	Not Needed
10. Did the teacher elicit descriptions of the analogy?	Thoroughly	Partially	Missing	Not Needed
11. Did the teacher record these descriptions?	Thoroughly	Partially	Missing	Not Needed

Phase Three: Personal Analogy

12. Did the teacher explain a personal analogy?	Thoroughly	Partially	Missing	Not Needed
13. Did the teacher ask students to become the "object"?	Thoroughly	Partially	Missing	Not Needed
14. Was the teacher able to get the students to state from a personal frame of reference:				
A. how they felt as the "object"?	Thoroughly	Partially	Missing	Not Needed
B. how they looked as the "object"?	Thoroughly	Partially	Missing	Not Needed
C. how they acted (kinesthetic involvement)?	Thoroughly	Partially	Missing	Not Needed
15. Did the teacher record the personal analogy description?	Thoroughly	Partially	Missing	Not Needed

Phase Four: Compressed Conflict

16. Did the teacher define compressed conflict?	Thoroughly	Partially	Missing	Not Needed
17. Did the teacher summarize the direct and personal analogies or ask the students to summarize them?	Thoroughly	Partially	Missing	Not Needed
18. Did the teacher elicit several compressed conflicts based on the materials from the direct and personal analogies?	Thoroughly	Partially	Missing	Not Needed
19. Were the students involved in the selection of one compressed conflict that was familiar to all of them?	Thoroughly	Partially	Missing	Not Needed

TEACHING ANALYSIS GUIDE FOR THE SYNECTICS MODEL (CREATING SOMETHING NEW)

Phase Five: New Direct Analogy

20. Did the teacher elicit several ideas containing the compressed conflict?	Thoroughly	Partially	Missing	Not Needed
21. Were the students involved in the selection of one idea that was familiar to everyone?	Thoroughly	Partially	Missing	Not Needed
22. Did the teacher elicit discussion of the direct analogy in terms of the compressed conflict?	Thoroughly	Partially	Missing	Not Needed

Phase Six: Reexamination of the Original Task

23. Did the teacher have the students describe the original task (idea) in terms of the last direct analogy?	Thoroughly	Partially	Missing	Not Needed
24. Did the students' descriptions indicate new dimensions or perceptions of the original task?	Thoroughly	Partially	Missing	Not Needed

Viewing the Lesson: Activity 2

In this section you are asked to read the demonstration transcript that follows, identifying the phases of the model and commenting on the lesson as an illustration of the model. On your own or with a group of your peers, note the occurrence of the phases and comment on the model as it is presented here. You may want to focus on the adequacy of each phase, the quality of the analogy, the degree of involvement, or the skillful moves the teacher made (or did not make).

Phase One	Adequate	Minimal	Not at All	Not Necessary
Phase Two	Adequate	Minimal	Not at All	Not Necessary
Phase Three	Adequate	Minimal	Not at All	Not Necessary
Phase Four	Adequate	Minimal	Not at All	Not Necessary
Phase Five	Adequate	Minimal	Not at All	Not Necessary
Phase Six	Adequate	Minimal	Not at All	Not Necessary

Analyzing the Lesson: Activity 3 (Optional)

View a live, taped, or filmed demonstration and analyze the lesson using the Teaching Analysis Guide. You can do this in two ways: either complete the Guide as the tape is viewed, or complete it afterward. If you are viewing the lesson in a group, you may want to divide the task of analysis with one or more of your colleagues, each person taking a particular phase or aspect of analysis. Duplicate as many copies of the Guide as are needed.

DEMONSTRATION TRANSCRIPT: SYNECTICS MODEL

The teacher has just completed directing the students through a series of stretching exercises doing direct analogies, personal analogies, and compressed conflicts.

T: WE HAVE BEEN GOING THROUGH OUR STRETCHING EXERCISES AND YOU SEEM TO HAVE IT. NOW I'M GOING TO DESCRIBE A CERTAIN CONDITION, AND THEN YOU'RE GOING TO WRITE ABOUT IT. WHAT I WANT YOU TO WRITE ABOUT IS WHAT BEING A PARENT MEANS TO YOU. I WANT YOU TO WRITE A SHORT PARAGRAPH ON IT. (Teacher passes out paper.) WHAT YOU HAVE JUST FINISHED DOING IS WRITING ABOUT WHAT BEING A PARENT MEANS TO YOU. DOES ANYONE WANT TO VOLUNTEER AND READ WHAT THEY HAVE? OKAY, VERONICA.

Phase One: **Describing the Present Condition**

S: BEING A PARENT MEANS, FIRST OF ALL, RESPONSIBILITY, PROBLEMS, HAPPINESS, AND SADNESS. A PARENT WOULD MOST LIKELY HAVE A FAMILY. THE FAMILY IS THE RESPONSIBILITY OF THE PARENT—TO RAISE THEM SO THAT THEY CAN BECOME INDEPENDENT. THE PARENTS CANNOT CHOOSE THEIR LIFE BUT ONLY HELP THEM BY THEIR OWN EXPERIENCE.

Students describe what they perceive being a parent is like.

T: ANYONE ELSE WANT TO SHARE WITH US WHAT THEY WROTE?

S: BEING A PARENT MEANS BEING RESTRICTED IN WHAT YOU DO. IT MEANS HAVING TO MAINTAIN RESPONSIBILITY TOWARD YOUR CHILDREN—ALWAYS HAVING TO WORRY ABOUT ALL THE NECESSITIES IN LIFE IN ORDER TO SURVIVE AND SO ON.

T: WHO ELSE WANTS TO SHARE? ED?

S: BEING A PARENT MEANS HAVING TO SACRIFICE YOUR OWN MONEY TOWARDS YOUR OWN CHILD. IT MEANS LOVING THEM, TAKING TENDER CARE OF THEM, IN ADDITION TO HELPING THEM THROUGH THEIR PROBLEMS IN LIFE. WHEN PUNISHMENT IS NEEDED, A GOOD PARENT KNOWS WHEN TO APPLY IT. IT MEANS BRINGING UP YOUR OWN CHILD THROUGH THE BEST TO THEIR OWN INDEPENDENCE.

T: WHO ELSE WANTS TO SHARE WITH US? TONY?

S: BEING A PARENT MEANS HAVING MANY RESPONSIBILITIES AND HAVING A FIRM GRIP ON THE CHILDREN AND HAVING THE RESPONSIBILITY TO SHOW THEM THAT THEY'LL HAVE LIBERTY WHEN THEY GROW UP. PARENTS HELP YOU THROUGH FINANCIAL PROBLEMS AND PROBLEMS AT SCHOOL.

T: ALL RIGHT. LINDA, DO YOU WANT TO SHARE WITH US?

S: IT'S A TOUGH JOB AND IT TAKES PATIENCE AND GENTLENESS, AND I FEEL THAT I'M NOT READY

TO BE A PARENT BECAUSE IT TAKES TIME. IT'S LIKE A CAREER. YOU LEARN; IT'S LIKE ON-THE-JOB TRAINING. EACH DAY YOU LEARN SOMETHING NEW THAT YOU DIDN'T KNOW BEFORE. YOU LEARN FROM TRIAL AND ERROR ABOUT YOUR CHILDREN. YOU LIKE HELPING A PERSON THROUGH LIFE. WHEN YOU'RE A PARENT, YOU'RE WILLING TO GIVE A PART OF YOURSELF TO SOMEBODY ELSE.

T: VERY GOOD. I WANT TO THANK ALL OF YOU THAT SHARED YOUR RESPONSES WITH US. THE NEXT THING WE WANT TO DO IS COMPARE. I WANT YOU TO THINK OF A PLANT THAT WOULD BE LIKE A PARENT. I'M GOING TO WRITE THEM UP HERE FOR YOU. WHAT PLANT IS LIKE A PARENT?

Phase Two: Direct Analogy
Teacher moves the students into analogies by asking for a direct analogy, specifying the category: plant. Teacher records students' contributions.

S: A REDWOOD TREE.

T: WHY?

Teacher asks for an explanation of the suggested analogy.

S: BECAUSE YOU LOOK UP TO IT; IT'S SOMETHING BIG TO YOU.

S: A CACTUS. SOMETIMES IT CAN BE HARD ON YOU, BUT ON THE INSIDE IT'S GOT REALLY IMPORTANT THINGS, LIKE WATER IN THE DESERT.

T: TONY?

S: A ROSEBUSH, BECAUSE IT PROTECTS. THE THORNS PROTECT THE ROSES FROM ANIMALS RIPPING OFF THE ROSES.

T: A PARENT IS LIKE WHAT MACHINE?

The category is changed from plant to machine.

S: A GENERATOR.

T: (writes on board) A GENERATOR. HOW IS THAT, ROBERT?

Teacher asks for elaboration of student's response.

S: A GENERATOR IS CONSTANTLY MOVING AND IT HELPS OTHER THINGS.

T: WHAT IF WE SAY A PARENT IS LIKE WHAT NON-LIVING OBJECT?

The category is changed again.

S: I KIND OF THINK OF A PARENT AS THE STEERING WHEEL OF A CAR; IT DIRECTS WHERE THE CAR IS GOING.

T: ANYBODY ELSE? I WANT YOU TO LOOK AT THESE WORDS HERE. CAN YOU SEE THE LIST, PATTY? I WANT YOU TO PICK ONE OF THESE WORDS THAT YOU LIKE BEST.

Teacher concludes Phase Two and moves into Phase Three by asking students to pick one of the words already generated. This word will be used for a personal analogy.

S: ROSEBUSH.

S: REDWOOD TREE.

T: DOES EVERYBODY AGREE WITH EITHER ONE OF THESE TWO? OK, SO LET'S SEE HOW MANY WANT REDWOOD TREE. HOW MANY WANT ROSEBUSH? LET'S WORK WITH ROSEBUSH THEN. WHAT I WANT YOU TO DO NOW IS TO BE THE ROSEBUSH. NOW, YOU ARE THE ROSEBUSH. HOW DO YOU LOOK?

Phase Three: Personal Analogy

Teacher requests that students state, from a personal frame of reference, how they look.

S: BEAUTIFUL.

T: DID I HEAR SOMEBODY SAY SOMETHING ELSE?

S: YES—THORNY.

T: THAT'S WHAT I THOUGHT I HEARD. OK, SO YOU LOOK THORNY. ANYBODY ELSE? YOU'RE IT. YOU ARE THE ROSEBUSH. HOW DO YOU LOOK?

S: COLORFUL.

T: COLORFUL. OK. HOW DO YOU FEEL?

S: PROTECTED.

T: HOW DO YOU FEEL PROTECTED?

S: WELL, NO ONE DARES TO GET NEAR ME WITHOUT GETTING STUCK BY THOSE THORNS.

S: STRICT, BECAUSE IT KEEPS THINGS AWAY FROM THE ROSES. IT PROTECTS YOU.

S: I WOULD FEEL KIND OF PROUD BECAUSE EVERY-ONE LOOKS AT ME.

T: PROUD.

S: I'D FEEL KIND OF POWERFUL. A ROSE IS SYM-BOLIC OF KINDNESS, BUT I'D FEEL POWERFUL BECAUSE I'D BE SMALL BUT NOTHING COULD REALLY TAKE ME AWAY.

T: OK, SO YOU'D FEEL KIND AND POWERFUL. ANY-BODY ELSE?

S: EVERLASTING. LIKE IF ONE ROSE DIES, AN-OTHER WILL TAKE ITS PLACE EVENTUALLY.

T: IF YOU DIE?

S: YES, IF SOMETHING HAPPENS TO ME, ANOTHER ROSE WILL GROW IN MY PLACE.

T: DOES ANYONE HAVE ANY MORE IDEAS ABOUT HOW YOU WOULD FEEL? WHAT DO YOU DO? OK, ROBERT. WE ARE TALKING ABOUT THIS ROSE-BUSH. WHAT DO YOU DO?

S: I HELP THE HUMANS AROUND ME BREATHE. I SUPPLY OXYGEN TO THEIR WORLD.

T: WHAT DO YOU DO IN YOUR ROSEBUSH? THINK OF YOURSELF. LINDA?

S: I FEEL LIKE HAPPINESS TO PEOPLE WHEN THEY LOOK AT ME.

T: YOU BRING HAPPINESS. IS THERE ONE ADJEC-TIVE THAT YOU CAN THINK OF THAT MIGHT COVER THAT? ANYBODY? I'LL PUT THAT HERE (writes).

T: OK, I HAVE ONE MORE THING. YOU ARE STILL THIS ROSEBUSH. IF YOU HAD A SECRET WISH, WHAT WOULD IT BE? LINDA?

S: THE WISH WOULD BE THAT I COULD BE EVER-LASTING, THAT I WOULD NEVER DIE. I WOULD ALWAYS BE BLOOMING ON THIS BUSH.

T: OK, YOU SAID "EVERLASTING" (writes). WERE YOU GOING TO SAY SOMETHING ELSE?

S: MY BUSH SAID NOTHING COULD DESTROY MY BEAUTY. NOTHING COULD HARM ME IN ANY WAY.

T: SO YOU WOULD BE INDESTRUCTIBLE.

S: OBVIOUSLY, I WISH THAT I COULD COMMUNI-CATE TO OTHER PLANTS LIKE ME.

Teacher asks how they feel as rosebushes.

Teacher asks for a justification.

By inserting the word "you," teacher redirects the students so that they *are* a rosebush.

Teacher directs the personal analogy to a kin-esthetic perspective.

Teacher records student responses.

T: OK, YOU WANT TO COMMUNICATE (writes). WE HAVE A GOOD LIST HERE. WHAT I WANT YOU TO DO NEXT IS TO LOOK AT YOUR LIST AND PICK TWO WORDS THAT OPPOSE EACH OTHER. HAS ANYONE SEEN TWO WORDS THAT ARE FIGHTING EACH OTHER?

S: THORNY AND BRING HAPPINESS.

T: I'LL PUT THAT THERE. ARE THERE ANY OTHERS? DO YOU SEE WORDS THAT ARE FIGHTING EACH OTHER—KIND OF LIKE OPPOSITES?

S: KIND AND POWERFUL?

T: KIND AND POWERFUL. HOW ARE THEY OPPOSITES?

S: IF YOU'RE KIND YOU'RE GENTLE, AND PEOPLE CAN SENSE THAT YOU'RE GENTLE; YOU CAN'T HARM ANYBODY. BEING POWERFUL, YOU'D HAVE A TENDENCY TO THINK YOU CAN DO SOMETHING TO HARM PEOPLE IN SOME MANNER.

S: I THINK THAT WOULD APPLY TO STRICT AND KIND.

T: DOES ANYONE SEE ANY MORE WORDS THAT YOU CAN PAIR TOGETHER, OR WOULD YOU FEEL COMFORTABLE CHOOSING FROM HERE?

S: I WAS THINKING OF EVERLASTING AND INDESTRUCTIVE.

S: THEY'RE BOTH THE SAME.

S: I KNOW, BUT IT FEELS LIKE THERE'S SOME DIFFERENCE, A SLIGHT DIFFERENCE BETWEEN THESE TWO WORDS—SOMETHING OPPOSING THEM.

T: YOU FEEL THAT THEY ARE NOT REALLY THE SAME—THEY'RE OPPOSITES?

S: YEAH.

S: BEAUTIFUL AND THORNY.

T: ARE YOU COMFORTABLE WITH THE LIST NOW? LET'S LOOK AT THE PAIRS WE HAVE NOW, AND I WANT YOU TO CHOOSE ONE OF THESE SETS.

OK, THIS IS IT—BEAUTIFUL AND THORNY. WE'RE GOING BACK NOW TO WHERE WE STARTED. REMEMBER, WE WERE DOING DIRECT ANALOGY. I WANT YOU TO THINK OF SOMETHING THAT IS BEAUTIFUL AND THORNY. ROBERT?

S: SOME GIRLS.

T: HOW IS THAT, ROBERT?

S: OK, ON THE OUTSIDE THEY APPEAR BEAUTIFUL. BUT WHILE THEY LOOK BEAUTIFUL, THEY COULD BE TAKING YOU FOR EVERYTHING YOU'VE GOT. THEY JUST PICK YOU.

T: ANOTHER ONE. DID SOMEONE THINK OF ANOTHER WORD? CAN YOU THINK OF A NONLIVING OBJECT THAT MAY BE BEAUTIFUL AND THORNY?

S: AN OVEN. IT CAN DO A LOT FOR YOU. IT COOKS FOOD AND GETS THINGS DONE A LOT QUICKER, BUT IF YOU MISHANDLE IT, IT CAN EVEN CATCH

Phase Four: Compressed Conflict

Teacher asks for a compressed conflict as an outgrowth of the personal analogies.

Teacher asks for explanation.

Teacher stops the listing of opposites by directing students to choose one.

Phase Five: New Direct Analogy

YOUR HOUSE ON FIRE AND BURN YOU AND CAUSE HARM.

T: OK, ANOTHER NON-LIVING OBJECT.

S: A BOOK. IT MIGHT HAVE AN ATTRACTIVE COVER, BUT THE NOVEL MIGHT BE LOUSY.

S: CORAL, BECAUSE CORALS ARE BEAUTIFUL. THEY HAVE POISON THAT, IF YOU TOUCH IT, IT CAN INJECT YOU AND MAKE YOU PARALYZED.

T: ANYBODY HAVE ANY MORE? YOU'VE GIVEN ME WORDS OR PHRASES OR THINGS THAT COULD BE BEAUTIFUL AND THORNY AT THE SAME TIME. WHAT I WANT YOU TO DO NOW IS TO THINK OF OUR ORIGINAL TASK. I WANT YOU TO USE THESE WORDS HERE. OUR ORIGINAL TASK WAS WHAT YOU THINK IT MEANS TO BE A PARENT. WHAT WE'LL BE DOING NOW IS USE SOME OF THESE WORDS HERE AND WRITE ABOUT IT. THE REASON I ASKED YOU TO WRITE FIRST IS THAT I WANT TO COMPARE WHAT YOU WRITE NOW AND SEE HOW DIFFERENT IT WILL BE FROM THE ORIGINAL ONE. USE SOME OF THESE WORDS HERE IN WRITING ON THE ORIGINAL TASK. PICK TWO WORDS FROM OUR LIST HERE AND WRITE ON OUR ORIGINAL TASK. THEY DON'T HAVE TO BE THE SAME FOR EACH. YOU CAN JUST PICK YOUR OWN. (students write)

OK, YOU HAVE FINISHED DOING THE ASSIGNMENT AGAIN. WHAT I WANT TO DO NOW IS GO BACK TO THE ORIGINAL PEOPLE THAT I ASKED BEFORE AND SEE HOW THEIR PARAGRAPHS HAVE CHANGED.

S: BEING A PARENT MEANS BEING RESTRICTED IN WHAT YOU DO. IT MEANS HAVING TO MAINTAIN RESPONSIBILITY TOWARD YOUR CHILDREN, ALWAYS HAVING TO WORRY ABOUT ALL THE NECESSITIES IN LIFE IN ORDER TO SURVIVE. AND THEN IN THE SECOND ONE, I DIDN'T WRITE A PARAGRAPH; I JUST USED TWO EXAMPLES. A BOOK, LIKE A PARENT, CONTAINS PAGES OF KNOWLEDGE AND WISDOM. FURNITURE SERVES A PURPOSE AS DOES A PARENT: IT'S FOR COMFORT. PARENTS COMFORT YOU WHEN YOU MAKE MISTAKES.

T: LET'S LISTEN TO ED.

S: BEING A PARENT MEANS HAVING TO SACRIFICE YOUR OWN MONEY FOR YOUR CHILD. IT MEANS LOVING THEM AND TAKING TENDER CARE OF THEM AND, IN ADDITION, HELPING THEM THROUGH THE PROBLEMS OF LIFE. WHEN PUNISHMENT IS NEEDED, A GOOD PARENT KNOWS WHEN TO APPLY IT, AND IT WILL HELP THEM TO END THEIR PROBLEMS. IT MEANS BRINGING THEM UP TO THEIR BEST AS AN INDEPENDENT PERSON.

T: LET'S HAVE YOUR SECOND.

Phase Six: Re-examination of the Original Task

Teacher returns students to the original task, directing them to use the compressed conflicts they have generated.

Teacher requests that students read their first and second writings.

S: A PAIR OF SHOES IN COMPARISON TO A PARENT. I WOULD SAY BOTH ARE STIFF BUT IMPORTANT; BOTH ARE BEAUTIFUL BUT RUGGED.

T: LINDA, WOULD YOU READ BOTH OF YOURS?

S: MINE ARE SORT OF LIKE HIS.

T: THAT'S OK. WHY DON'T YOU READ IT FOR US?

S: THE FIRST ONE WAS: BEING A PARENT TAKES PATIENCE AND GENTLENESS, AND IT'S LIKE A CAREER. YOU GO THROUGH TRIAL AND ERROR AND ON-THE-JOB TRAINING. THE BOSS IS THE PARENT. TO BE A PARENT YOU MUST BE WILLING TO GIVE TO OTHERS. AND THEN THE OTHER: IT WOULD BE LIKE AN OVEN. ON THE INSIDE IT'S HOT AND ANGRY, AND YET YOU KNOW IT'S THERE TO HELP YOU. THEN IT COULD BE COLD OR UNFEELING TOWARD YOU. SHOES—HOW THEY COULD BE NICE LOOKING ON THE OUTSIDE, AND YET ON THE INSIDE THEY COULD HURT YOU OR COULD BE JUST THE OPPOSITE AND HELP YOU.

T: OK. VERY GOOD. THE PURPOSE OF WRITING YOUR PARAGRAPH THE SECOND TIME IS FOR YOU TO SEE HOW IT IS MORE CREATIVE THAN YOUR FIRST (NOT THAT YOUR FIRST ONE WASN'T). BECAUSE YOU HAVE BEEN GOING THROUGH THE EXERCISES, IT'S MORE CREATIVE. YOU ARE USING WORDS AND REALLY PUTTING THEM IN A DIFFERENT CONTEXT. THIS IS THE END OF OUR LESSON, AND I WANT TO THANK ALL OF YOU. YOU WERE REALLY TERRIFIC.

Teacher concludes by restating the purpose of the lesson and praising the students on their improvement.

Component III

PLANNING AND PEER TEACHING

In this component, you will plan a lesson using Strategy One (Creating Something New), teach this lesson to a small group of peers, and then evaluate the lesson using the Teaching Analysis Guide. The activities in this component include:

I. Planning the lesson
Step 1. choosing a topic and a mode of expression
Step 2. determining educational objectives
Step 3. preparing examples
Step 4. completing the Planning Guide

II. Peer teaching the lesson

III. Analyzing the peer teaching using the Teaching Analysis Guide

IV. Microteaching: teaching the same lesson to a small group of students and evaluating their performance

We have selected Strategy One because we have found that it works well with students of all ages. We feel that if you can plan using Strategy One, you should be able to transfer those skills to other variations of the Synectics Model. The advantage of Creating Something New is its open-endedness: there is never a right "right answer" that must be found. Consequently, it is not bound to any particular content area; it can be used with all subject areas, as well as with personal problems and issues of social concern.

In our discussion of Step 1 (choosing a topic and a mode of expression), we make suggestions concerning topics, modes of expression, the use of evocative questions, and the analysis of metaphorical activity. Our intention is to elaborate Synectics theory, focusing on classroom practices. If you already have in mind a topic to teach and you feel comfortable that you can readily identify the mode of expression, you may want to skip this step and proceed to Step 2, the determination of educational objectives. However, at some point you should return to the discussion of Step 1. It will assist you in long-term curriculum planning and help you make choices for other lessons based on Synectics.

After you plan the lesson, you will teach it to a small group of your colleagues. Select a topic that is appropriate for adults, but, if you wish, one that may also be used when you microteach the lesson. Our only caution is that you may need to allow more time for stretching exercises when using the model with students. If you and your colleagues have completed the walk-through of the model and the stretching exercises contained in the Taking Theory Into Action section, you are more prepared for metaphoric activity than a group of students in a microteaching situation. Following the peer teaching, we ask you to complete the Teaching Analysis Guide, which provides guidelines for self-evaluation. We suggest that you use the Guide again after microteaching and compare your two teaching experiences. As you incorporate the Synectics Model into your classroom, you will find it useful to analyze your teaching from time to time.

CHOOSING A TOPIC AND A MODE OF EXPRESSION

Synectics training can be applied to many different learning situations in the classroom. Topics may be found in traditional subject areas or in nonacademic areas. Synectics can be used in language arts to expand the writing program; the metaphoric activity will bring new vitality to student expository and fictional writing. Synectics procedures help students increase their awareness of the world and become more vivid describers of what they see each day. In addition, Synectics can be a method for teaching autobiography, biography, and character analysis in literature. Asking students to put themselves into the feelings and actions of others will help them perceive others in new ways. By metaphorically comparing their observations and insights with those of writers, students will be able to understand more about their own experience. Synectics can also be used as the basis for improvisational drama and for expanding the imagination of the participants. Especially important here is the teacher's willingness to engage in verbal play of fancy. Finally, Synectics can be part of a language-development program. Synectics' emphasis on language—choosing the exact word that will epitomize the process of innovation or inspiration—is important in all modes of communication in the language arts. Understanding the effect of words has implications for all media and for advertising. Synectics procedures are particularly useful if teachers want to duplicate the group creativity that is often a part of creating the commercials we see, hear, and read each day.

Synectics allows students to make their own connections in the sciences. Gordon believes that traditional science teaching, which uses the inductive method, is too concerned with the "correct" answer and not concerned enough with the process of science.[1] He wants students to increase their depth of understanding about facts that they observe in the world around them, adding these facts to ones they already know in order to hypothesize about new problems. In using Synectics in general science, biology, physics, and chemistry, the teacher can emphasize hypothesis formation, hypothesis testing or workability, the use of discovered information to link one hypothesis to another, and finally the formulation of theories about how scientific phenomena are connected. Synectics is prepared to let students fail in problem solving in order that they understand that the real process of scientific discovery is often filled with numerous mistakes before the sought-after inspiration or innovation occurs.

The use of analogy can help students stretch their imagination to understand and connect scientific phenomena. Often, scientists and mathematicians express their ideas metaphorically before they achieve actual scientific proof. For example, Pasteur described vaccination as a "safe attack" long before he perfected the method. Records of scientific methodology are replete with similar examples.

In the teaching of mathematics, Synectics can be used to explore the ideas underlying mathematical principles. Theoretical mathematicians often express their ideas about the underlying principles of formulas in metaphysical language. The use of metaphor can help students express concepts in math rather than just calculating problems.

The social sciences are the curricula areas concerned with human problems. Courses in economics, history, political science, and law are adaptable to the needs of adolescents confronting problems of their own maturity and of the society in which they will soon be expected to assume an adult role. Through the use of metaphor, students can explore the ideas and values of society. Metaphoric activity will help students move beyond stereotypic views of such abstract ideas as democracy, prejudice, poverty, national debt, and legal right. It will extend their perceptions in the social sciences beyond superficial analysis.

Gordon's original work stresses an interdisciplinary approach—the use of metaphorical activity to combine learning areas so that students can see connections among the vast quantities of information presented in classrooms. For example, the social concept of revolution is analyzed in terms of its likenesses to and differences from a volcano. Combining concepts across the fine arts, the language arts, science and math, and the social sciences can help students connect discrete bits of information with broad theories or recurring social themes. Metaphorical processes also allow students to evaluate seemingly unconnected information. In this way, they will have a stronger view of the connections among ideas in modern thought. Many young people find their ideas fractured and view the world as a series of unconnected events. More techniques for helping students integrate their knowledge are needed in schools. Synectics offers students insight into alternative ways of coping with their personal problems and interpersonal relationships. Thus, it can be used as a technique for personal growth. By using these techniques in the classroom, students build empathy listening to one another and involving themselves in the analogies. Direct analogy is an unthreatening way to explore a problem with a student or a class of students. If a problem is to be

---

[1]William Gordon, *The Metaphorical Way of Knowing* (Cambridge, Mass.: Synectics, Inc., 1970), p. 57.

probed deeply, all of the metaphoric techniques should be used. The group process of Synectics is equally concerned with individual insights and knowledge from group processes.

Formulating the Topic

Topics for Synectics lessons can be formulated in a variety of ways. Concepts may be used as topics—for example, friendship, trust, government, zero. Interpersonal problems may be used as topics—for example, what do we do about the shy, withdrawn person? In the latter case, the purpose is both to understand the concept "shy, withdrawn person" and to come up with a plan of action for dealing with the problem. Specific behavioral incidents or problem situations that occur in the classroom can also be used as topics for Synectics. Broad social issues and problems make excellent material for Synectics lessons—for example, the farm workers' strike, United States arms policy, busing, and national medical insurance. Synectics originated as a way to solve industrial-design problems, such as creating a can that could be opened without an opener. Teachers can use Synectics to help students solve such design problems as making a set for the school play, painting a picture, or arranging the classroom. In the biological and physical sciences, problems involving either the creation of things or the discovery of principles and explanations can be formulated as topics for Synectics lessons.

The same theme or idea can be formulated in more than one way. Prejudice, for example, can be dealt with as a concept, an interpersonal problem, a social issue, or even a creative-design task. What you want as the outcome of the lesson has much to do with how you formulate the task, and vice versa. The instructions you give the students depend on the task you choose for them. Similarly, the nature of the metaphor—whether to use nouns, verbs, or phrases—depends on whether you are aiming for a solution, a description, or a product.

EXERCISE 1

In the spaces below, list four themes or situations from your current teaching assignment that might be appropriate for a peer teaching lesson. Then formulate them into a topic for a Synectics lesson. Try to formulate two different tasks for each theme.

Theme/Situation	Formulation 1	Formulation 2
1.		
2.		
3.		
4.		

Modes of Expression

All of the examples of Synectics in this training system use discussion and a writing experience as the mode of expression. That is, the metaphoric activity is verbal, and the original problem or task and its reconceptualization are described in written form. It is important to recognize that the products of Synectics lessons need not always be in writing. Other choices may spark greater creativity. The possible modes of expression include:

1. writing
2. verbal (oral) interchange
3. object/physical model
4. graphic/painting/drawing
5. role playing/creative dramatics
6. behavior change

The mode of expression you select will depend on your purposes. For example, if you are using Synectics to explore social or behavior problems, you may look for behavior changes before and after the Synectics activity. It is also interesting to select modes of expression that contrast with the original topic—such as having students paint a picture of prejudice or discrimination. The concept is abstract, but the mode of expression is concrete. The final choice of a mode of expression is governed by your particular objectives for the lesson and your particular teaching situation and students.

EXERCISE 2

Go back to the topics you formulated in Exercise 1. For each formulation, select a mode of expression. Try to use all the possible modes of expression.

From the topics you have developed, select *one* that you will use in peer teaching, and determine the mode of expression you will use. Consider the limitations that you may face in peer teaching, as these may affect both your choice of topics and mode of expression. When you have decided on the topic and mode of expression, record these in Part I of the Planning Guide.

DETERMINING EDUCATIONAL OBJECTIVES

Synectics Models can be employed toward several ends. They can be used (1) to increase students' understanding, (2) to link the knowledge in different subject areas, and (3) to help students learn about the formation of hypotheses. Although teachers may employ Synectics for a wide variety of educational purposes, the classroom procedures are essentially the same each time. Some of the educational purposes that might be considered are:

1. creativity
2. empathy

3. new attitudes or positions

4. problem solving

5. making a product design or plan

6. deeper meaning

7. behavior

8. deeper levels of metaphoric activity

Many of these purposes are accomplished in the course of the model. Others may require designing follow-up educational activities. Look now at the topic you have selected. Determine your broad objective(s) for this topic, and list three specific objectives. Record these in Part II of the Planning Guide.

EXERCISE 3 (OPTIONAL)

With a group of peers, generate a list of specific objectives as they would appear in Synectics for each of the eight educational purposes listed above. An alternative activity would be to divide into small groups, and compare and contrast the list of goals each group prepared.

PREPARING EXAMPLES OF STRETCHING EXERCISES AND ANALOGIES

The major planning activity is the formulation of the topic and mode of expression. The teacher can also plan stretching exercises and evocative questions to assist the students in working through the first direct analogies. Beyond this, the analogies and descriptions emerge from the students' comments. The teacher functions in a supportive role, encouraging students as they move through the creative process. The critical aspect of planning the direct analogy is to suggest a category that structures as much conceptual distance as possible between the original topic and the direct analogy. (In other words, we want to stretch the students' imaginations as much as possible.)

It is also important to remember whether you want students to devise a plan of action, suggest new behavior, or describe something. Direct analogies should be parallel in form to the original problem or topic. For example, if students are to suggest ways to improve relationships with their parents, the direct analogy should be an idea that includes a problem-solving process (such as opening a locked window or planning a trip) rather than a single concept (a window or trip).

During stretching exercises (and subsequent metaphoric activity in the model), the major points to remember are to provide a definition and examples of each type of analogy and, more important, to plan follow-up questions that will help the students extend their description of each metaphor they use.

Now complete Parts III and IV of the Planning Guide.

PLANNING GUIDE FOR THE SYNECTICS MODEL (CREATING SOMETHING NEW)

I. Topic and Mode of Expression

    1. Identify and describe (briefly) the topic.

    2. What mode of expression will you have the students use? (Check one.)

        _____ writing

        _____ verbal (oral) interchange

        _____ object/physical model

        _____ graphic/painting/drawing

        _____ role play/creative dramatics

        _____ behavior change

II. Educational Objectives

    3. In the chart below, identify the type of topic you have selected and your educational purpose(s) with respect to that topic.

Type of Topic	Educational Purpose(s)
_____ 1. concept	_____ 1. creativity
_____ 2. intrapersonal problem	_____ 2. empathy
_____ 3. interpersonal problem	_____ 3. new attitudes or positions
_____ 4. intergroup problem	_____ 4. problem solving
_____ 5. social or behavioral problem	_____ 5. making a product, a design, or a plan
_____ 6. social issue/social action	_____ 6. a deeper meaning
_____ 7. design task	_____ 7. behavior
	_____ 8. deeper levels of metaphoric activity

    4. List three behavioral objectives that you expect students to accomplish in this lesson.

III. Stretching Exercises

    5. Define and give examples of each of the three types of analogies as you might explain them to students.

Direct Analogy:

Personal Analogy:

Compressed Conflict:

6. List the stretching exercises you will use to help students loosen up and become more familiar with metaphoric activity. For each one, add several evocative questions that will help students extend their description of the analogy.

Direct Analogy:

Personal Analogy:

Compressed Conflict:

IV. Planning for Direct Analogies

7. Characterize your topic. (Circle the appropriate words.)

_____ Organic/Inorganic

_____ Concrete/Abstract

8. What types of direct analogies would you suggest for this topic?

V. Phases of the Model

9. Write your instructions and opening move for each phase of the model.

Phase One: Description

Phase Two: Direct Analogy

Phase Three: Personal Analogy

Phase Four: Compressed Conflict

Phase Five: New Direct Analogy

Phase Six: Reexamination of the Original Task

ANALYZING THE PEER TEACHING LESSON

The questions in the Teaching Analysis Guide are designed to remind you to check that important features of the model are taken into account in your peer teaching. Feel free to comment on other aspects of the lesson and to help the teacher reflect on aspects in the lesson pointed out in the Teaching Analysis Guide. Concentrate on the use of analogies and the stimulation of metaphoric activity! Duplicate as many copies of the Guide as may be needed to analyze the peer teaching and microteaching of all members of the group.

TEACHING ANALYSIS GUIDE FOR THE SNYECTICS MODEL (CREATING SOMETHING NEW)

This Guide is designed to help you analyze the process of teaching as you practice the Reception Model of Concept Attainment. The analysis focuses on aspects of teaching that are important to the syntax of the model, the teacher's role, and specific teaching skills.

The Guide consists of a series of questions and phrases. As you observe a practice session (whether peer teaching or microteaching), analyze the teaching using the rating scale that appears opposite each question and statement. The scale uses the following items:

Thoroughly. This item signifies that the teacher engaged in the behavior to the point where students were responding comfortably and fluently. Appropriateness varies from situation to situation.

Partially. This item signifies that the teacher engaged in appropriate behavior, but not as thoroughly as possible. There is some doubt about whether the students are responding fully.

Missing. The teacher did not engage in the behavior; there appears to be a loss in student response or probably will be one.

Not Needed. The teacher did not explicitly manifest the behavior, but there is no loss. Either the behavior was included in others or the students began to respond appropriately without being led to.

For each question or statement in the Guide, circle the term that best describes the teacher's behavior.

Phase One: Description

1. Did the teacher elicit ideas from students about the topic?

Thoroughly Partially Missing Not Needed

Phase Two: Direct Analogy

2. Did the teacher define a direct analogy?

Thoroughly Partially Missing Not Needed

3. Did the teacher specify the type of analogy, such as nonliving or machine?

Thoroughly Partially Missing Not Needed

4. Did the teacher elicit analogies?

Thoroughly Partially Missing Not Needed

5. Did the category of analogy appropriately contrast the topic? (For example, if the topic was a living thing, such as a shy child, was the category of analogies nonliving things, such as a machine?)

Thoroughly Partially Missing Not Needed

6. Did the teacher elicit several analogies?

Thoroughly Partially Missing Not Needed

7. If necessary, did the teacher ask students to clarify their suggested analogies?

Thoroughly Partially Missing Not Needed

8. Did the students select one analogy to work with?

Thoroughly Partially Missing Not Needed

81

TEACHING ANALYSIS GUIDE FOR THE SNYECTICS MODEL (CREATING SOMETHING NEW)

9. Was the analogy familiar to all the students?	Thoroughly	Partially	Missing	Not Needed
10. Did the teacher elicit descriptions of the analogy?	Thoroughly	Partially	Missing	Not Needed
11. Did the teacher record these descriptions?	Thoroughly	Partially	Missing	Not Needed

Phase Three: Personal Analogy

12. Did the teacher explain a personal analogy?	Thoroughly	Partially	Missing	Not Needed
13. Did the teacher ask students to become the "object"?	Thoroughly	Partially	Missing	Not Needed
14. Was the teacher able to get the students to state from a personal frame of reference:				
A. how they felt as the "object"?	Thoroughly	Partially	Missing	Not Needed
B. how they looked as the "object"?	Thoroughly	Partially	Missing	Not Needed
C. how they acted (kinesthetic involvement)?	Thoroughly	Partially	Missing	Not Needed
15. Did the teacher record the personal analogy description?	Thoroughly	Partially	Missing	Not Needed

Phase Four: Compressed Conflict

16. Did the teacher define compressed conflict?	Thoroughly	Partially	Missing	Not Needed
17. Did the teacher summarize the direct and personal analogies or ask the students to summarize them?	Thoroughly	Partially	Missing	Not Needed
18. Did the teacher elicit several compressed conflicts based on the materials from the direct and personal analogies?	Thoroughly	Partially	Missing	Not Needed
19. Were the students involved in the selection of one compressed conflict that was familiar to all of them?	Thoroughly	Partially	Missing	Not Needed

Phase Five: New Direct Analogy

20. Did the teacher elicit several ideas containing the compressed conflict?	Thoroughly	Partially	Missing	Not Needed

TEACHING ANALYSIS GUIDE FOR THE SNYECTICS MODEL (CREATING SOMETHING NEW)

21. Were the students involved in the selection of one idea that was familiar to everyone?	Thoroughly	Partially	Missing	Not Needed
22. Did the teacher elicit discussion of the direct analogy in terms of the compressed conflict?	Thoroughly	Partially	Missing	Not Needed

Phase Six: Reexamination of the Original Task

23. Did the teacher have the students describe the original task (idea) in terms of the last direct analogy?	Thoroughly	Partially	Missing	Not Needed
24. Did the students' descriptions indicate new dimensions or perceptions of the original task?	Thoroughly	Partially	Missing	Not Needed

AFTER PEER TEACHING: MICROTEACHING

Peer teaching was an opportunity to "walk through" the pattern of a Synectics lesson to foster creativity in students. The Teaching Analysis Guide should have helped you identify areas of your understanding and performance that need further development. Aside from the specifics of the Guide, we would encourage you to reflect intuitively on your peer teaching experience. Did you feel that you were successful in framing evocative questions to start the metaphoric experience? After stretching exercises, were you able to move through the levels of metaphor? Were you satisfied with your students' creative product at the end of the lesson? Were you able to accept and employ the role of facilitator in helping students develop metaphors leading to a creative product?

As you now prepare for your microteaching, identify aspects of the Synectics strategy you would like to improve upon. Usually, this means assuming more of a facilitating role as the students work through the creative process, helping them achieve greater conceptual distance in their metaphors, and evaluating their metaphoric descriptions. We suggest that you mentally "walk through" another series of metaphors before microteaching.

At this point, you have a choice: You may microteach with a class of students using Strategy One (Creating Something New), or you may complete Component IV.

If you choose to microteach, we recommend that you record your lesson on an audio-tape so that you can reflect on the lesson afterwards. Students will respond differently from your peers. It is a good idea to evaluate the lesson with the Teaching Analysis Guide. You may also want to share the experience with your colleagues and receive their comments and suggestions.

The fourth and last component in this model suggests how to adapt the model to an entire class and how to incorporate other models with Synectics. The emphasis in your training in the model will now gradually shift from mastering the basic elements to designing and applying the model in the classroom.

Component IV

ADAPTING
THE MODEL

The first Synectics strategy—Creating Something New—was developed in Components I, II, and III. In this component, we shall present some of Gordon's suggestions for working with the second strategy—Making the Strange Familiar. We will also discuss Gordon's ideas concerning the use of programmed material with Synectics. Finally, we shall discuss how Synectics can be used with other models of teaching.

Synectics belongs to the personal family of teaching models, and as such it is concerned with individual growth and development. The expansion of Synectics into the classroom through curriculum transformations, long-range planning, and combination with other models offers potential for developing student interests. Synectics can be used as a personal-growth strategy apart from curriculum developments, as a strategy for the development of personality, self-awareness, and greater discipline within the classroom. Using the metaphor technique, students explore personal problems while maintaining some distance from them.

Synectics as a Personal Growth Strategy

In using personal-growth techniques in the classroom, the teacher builds empathy by instructing the students to listen to the speaker and then respond. Listening means more than just hearing; it means being able to respond to the subtleties of the speaker's description. Achieving this, the students or leader ask evocative questions that will extend the initial metaphorical description. The use of direct analogy or personal analogy provides a mutually understood beginning for communication.

In describing the function of metaphor, Gordon says, "The use of metaphor provides a device for absorbing both the content and feeling of another person's statement so that an understanding of the implications that underlie what others say and do develops from the listening process."[1] Gordon suggests several procedures for working with personal problems or discipline problems or trying to increase communication:

1. Each group member writes down what animal he or she would like to be.

2. In turn, group members read their descriptions. Using evocative questions to prompt more description, the teacher extends the metaphors until the students try on all of the possibilities.

3. After each member has presented an analogy, the group discusses the metaphor from a different point of view:

   A. Was the metaphor candid?

   B. Did the evocative questions help?

   C. Did the speaker feel threatened? If so, did the evocative questions alleviate this?

   D. Did the speaker find out anything more that he or she had not known before?[2]

Using direct analogy or personal analogy can be an unthreatening way to explore a problem with a student or a class. If a problem is to be probed in any depth, all of the metaphoric techniques can be used. Failure to extend the metaphor can leave the student unaware of possibilities and nuances in the idea. The role of the teacher is to guide exploration to its fullest, but also to oversee the discussion and stop it at the most judicious point. Too much exploration can be as harmful as too little. We caution, further, that all class or group members must be aware of the goal and that manipulation of persons should be avoided at all times.

The teacher's concern in using the group process of Synectics with personal problems is equally with individual insights and knowledge of group processes. We would like to offer some summary comments about using Synectics as a personal-growth strategy in discipline or behavior problems as well as in organizational problems within groups.

1. The direct analogy should be used first. It will be accepted and used most readily by the students. Some persons may, at first, hesitate to identify personally with an animal or object.[3]

2. Compressed conflict usually grows naturally out of honest direct analogy

[1] William Gordon, *The Metaphorical Way of Knowing and Learning* (Cambridge, Mass.: Synectics Education Systems, 1970), p. 183. © W.J.J. Gordon. Additional information can be obtained from Synectics Education Systems, 121 Brattle St., Cambridge, Mass. 02138.

[2] *Ibid.*, p. 188.

[3] *Ibid.*, p. 202.

or personal analogy. Therefore, there is no need to try to get participants to form compressed conflicts. If they do not arise naturally, the problem has not provided sufficient engagement.[4]

3. In the evaluation of the metaphor, the amount of conceptual distance or strain in the metaphor will determine the honesty of the responses. An analogy with strain, distance, and obliqueness opens communication and enhances the group's ability to function.[5]

4. Having allowed the analogy to develop, the teacher needs to ask evocative questions that will help the students establish parallels between the analogy and the real situation. It is best if students can see connections on their own, but teacher guidance is needed if students seem unwilling or unable to make the connections.[6]

CURRICULAR POSSIBILITIES AND ADAPTATIONS

Curricula transformations with Synectics involve Strategy Two, Making the Strange Familiar. This strategy is useful for interdisciplinary work and for approaching complex ideas in a way that can easily be absorbed by students. Comparing the phases of the two strategies, we see that the chief distinction between Creating Something New and Making the Strange Familiar is the use of metaphor.

Phase One: Description of Present Condition	Phase Two: Direct Analogy	Phase Three: Personal Analogy
Teacher gets students' description of situation or topic as they see it now.	Students suggest direct analogies, select one, and explore (describe) it further.	Students "become" the analogy they selected in Phase Two.
Phase Four: Compressed Conflict	**Phase Five: Direct Analogy**	**Phase Six: Reexamination of the Original Task**
Students take their descriptions from Phases Two and Three, suggest several compressed conflicts, and choose one.	Students generate and select another direct analogy, based on the compressed conflict.	Teacher gets students to move back to original task or problem and utilize the last analogy and/or the entire Synectics experience.

[4] *Ibid.*, p. 188.
[5] *Ibid.*, p. 202.
[6] *Ibid.*

Phase One: Substantive Input	Phase Two: Direct Analogy	Phase Three: Personal Analogy
Teacher provides information on new topic.	Teacher suggests direct analogy and asks students to describe the analogy.	Teacher gets students to "become" the direct analogy.

Phase Four: Comparing Analogies	Phase Five: Explaining Differences	Phase Six: Exploration
Students identify and explain the points of similarity between the new material and the direct analogy.	Students explain where the analogy doesn't fit.	Students re-explore the original topic on its own terms.

Phase Seven:
Generating Analogy

Students provide their own direct analogy and explore the similarities and differences.

The purposes of the strategy are clear. In moving from Phase One to Phase Seven, the student draws on past experience and knowledge combined with metaphorical activity to master new ideas. To accomplish this end, Gordon has prepared interdisciplinary curriculum material. A sample of this material is included here. As you read through it, notice how he combines music, English, math, fine arts, social science, and physical sciences.

You've seen volcanos on TV or in the movies. When volcanos burst and erupt they have been known to bury whole cities. What goes on inside them to make them so violent? Let's use comparisons to begin to understand what makes a volcano BLOW UP!

The earth is not a hard, solid ball of rock. Only the earth's crust is hard. Inside, the earth is filled with magma which is hot, liquid rock. What else do you know that has a hard surface and a soft inside?

_____

Explain how your hard outside, soft inside thing is like the earth. _____

_____

_____

_____

_____

The magma (hot, liquid rock) shifts about and pushes against the earth's crust from underneath. When the magma finds a weak spot in the earth's crust, it shoots through this weak spot. How is the magma in the earth like the blood in the human body?

_____

_____

_____

_____

_____

How is a cut on the human body like the eruption of a volcano?

_____

_____

(There are more lines on the next page.)

W. J. Gordon and Tony Poze, *Strange and Familiar VI,* pp. 21-26. Reprinted by permission of Synectics Education Systems, Cambridge, Mass. © W. J. J. Gordon. Additional information can be obtained from Synectics Education Systems, 121 Brattle St., Cambridge, Mass. 02138.

_____

_____

_____

You might think a volcano is quite unlike a bleeding cut on the human body. What are the differences between a bleeding cut and a volcano? _____

_____

_____

_____

_____

_____

_____

Find an example of your own. What in the world of living things is like a volcano?

_____

Describe how your example acts like a volcano. _____

_____

_____

_____

_____

The American Revolution is an example from history that can be looked at in terms of a volcano. You will remember that the thirteen English Colonies in America were unhappy about the way England governed them. The taxes were too high, for instance, and the Colonists weren't

allowed to help make the laws they had to obey. The colonists showed
their dissatisfaction by refusing to buy English products, by throwing rocks
at the English soldiers, and by dumping English tea into Boston Harbor.
How is the colonists' dissatisfaction with the English like the magma building up pressure under the earth's crust?

_____

_____

_____

_____

_____

In 1776 the colonists became so dissatisfied with the English soldiers and the laws that they seized guns and fought for the right to govern
themselves. How is the actual eruption of a volcano like the fighting stage
of the Revolutionary War?

_____

_____

_____

_____

_____

On the first page of this Unit, there is a drawing of a volcano. All
the parts are labelled. The drawing on the next page is exactly the same as
the one on page 120, but the label boxes are empty. Use what you have discovered about the Revolutionary War to help you label this volcano drawing.
Be sure to write something in every box.

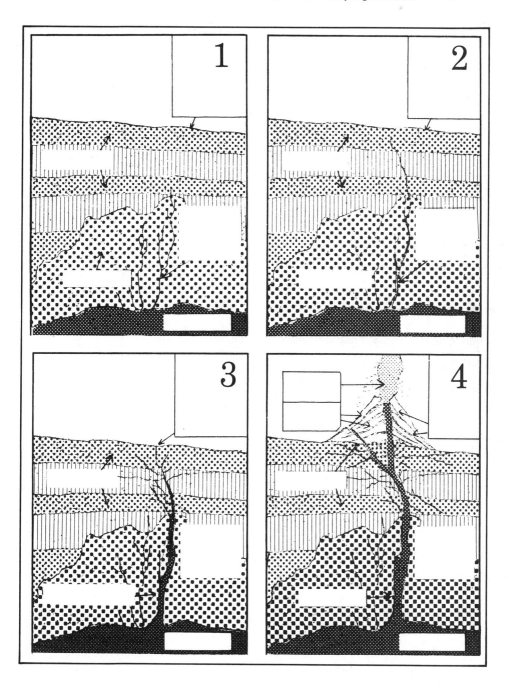

How is the Revolutionary War and its causes different from the causes and eruption of a volcano?

_____

_____

_____

_____

_____

_____

_____

✳✳✳   NOW TO BE LESS SERIOUS . . .   **✳✳✳**

If the English army had fought with LAWNMOWERS, what would the AMERICAN COLONISTS have been?_____

Explain your answer:_____

_____

_____

_____

If there were a WHIP-CREAM VOLCANO, what would be the CHERRY ON TOP?_____

How come?_____

_____

_____

_____

In this part of BLOW UP, you will be using what you know about the American Revolution and volcanos to understand music and art.   You will listen to a part of a musical composition by Richard Wagner.

Richard Wagner was a major composer of operas in Germany in the nineteenth century.   The music to play now is the famous overture to Wagner's opera, Tannhauser which introduces the listeners to some of the melodies in the opera itself.

In this overture Wagner creates a broad, heavy sound with lots of brass instruments.   Listen to the melodies in the first two minutes of the record.

(THE RECORD IS PLAYED.)

Turn to the volcano drawing you labelled.   As you listen to this piece of music by Wagner, look out for parts of the music which remind you of the dissatisfaction that led to the American Revolution.

(THE RECORD IS PLAYED AGAIN.)

As you listen to the Wagner selection for the last time, start a painting or drawing of the American Revolution.   Use the next page for your picture.   It need not have recognizable people or things in it.   Be as wild as you like!   When you have finished your picture, use the lines below to describe the ways Wagner's music is like your picture.

(THE RECORD IS PLAYED FOR THE LAST TIME.)

_____

_____

_____

_____

_____

_____

_____

The usual Synectics pattern described in the material to now has been teacher speak—student respond. Gordon has developed programmed material for Synectics. This is curricular transformation that is possible if teachers follow some simple guidelines outlined in Gordon's material. The following unit describes programmed instruction that can transform curriculum to meet individual student needs.

ᴖUnit Seven

This Unit in TEACHING IS LISTENING will demonstrate how NOT to write an open-ended programmed Unit. Although testing will illuminate the inadequacies of any given Unit, it is much more efficient (to say nothing about being more heartening) to find positive results when you test. You will see a typical product of a well-meaning, intelligent teacher who having made a quick study of some Synectics materials tried to apply the metaphorical approach to learning. You must understand that this teacher is a good person who believes in the infinite imagination of his students. In fact, he believes his students have so much imagination that they can read his mind and follow his 'hidden', implied instructions.

Keep in mind as you read through this Unit that (1) it was designed to be the first presentation of Synectics to students and (2) we have purposely highlighted the counter-productive programming that the teacher included.

SOMETIMES WHEN YOU BEGIN SOMETHING
NEW YOU FIND YOURSELF HOLDING BACK, AFRAID
OF MAKING A MISTAKE OR OF BEING LAUGHED AT
FOR EXPRESSING A STRANGE WAY OF LOOKING AT
SOMETHING. ALL IT TAKES IS A LITTLE COURAGE
TO EXPRESS IT.

LET'S TALK ABOUT COURAGE. OBVIOUS
EXAMPLES OF COURAGE WOULD BE —
A SOLDIER
A FIREMAN
A TRAPEZE ARTIST
a POW
a cop on the take

W. J. Gordon and Tony Poze, *Teaching Is Listening*, pp. 65-72. Reprinted by permission of Synectics Education Systems, Cambridge, Mass. © W. J. J. Gordon. Additional information can be obtained from Synectics Education Systems, 121 Brattle St., Cambridge, Mass. 02138.

The Unit has just begun and the programming already has created possible problems for the student. In the first place, students are being kept in the dark as to what the Unit is about. Though the lesson is supposed to be an introduction to the Synectics use of metaphor, for all the students know the lesson is about "courage."

In the second place, there are some lines at the end of the list of "examples of courage." What are they for? The un-written instruction is that the students are to supply their own examples to complete the list. Since there is no <u>written</u> instruction to do so, what is the basis for confidence that students will understand what is intended?

ALL OF THESE EXAMPLES OF COURAGE ARE OK, BUT THEY DO NOT OFFER MUCH OF A CHALLENGE AND IT DOESN'T TAKE MUCH COURAGE TO EXPRESS THEM. TO GET A NEW IDEA OF COURAGE, LOOK FOR A NEW KIND OF EXAMPLE OF IT — NOT A HEROIC PERSON OR PUBLIC FIGURE, NOT EVEN A HUMAN BEING! GO TO THE INSECT WORLD FOR A MORE SURPRISING EXAMPLE.

WHAT INSECT IS COURAGE? _army ants_

YOU HAVE JUST MADE A DIRECT ANALOGY — YOU DIRECTLY COMPARED ONE THING WITH ANOTHER. NOW FIGURE OUT WHY OR HOW THIS INSECT IS COURAGE. _they are built like tanks and they have courage to eat anything in their path._

Unfortunately the Unit's directions are so ambiguous that there can be no security that students actually "HAVE JUST MADE A DIRECT AN-ALOGY." Furthermore, if they did produce a "DIRECT ANALOGY" they are liable to feel that they have been tricked into it. It is imperative that students know exactly where they are going and what should be happening. Surprises of the kind that are here simply make for lack of confidence. If the purpose of the Unit is to introduce the basic Synectics mechanisms, then it fails because of the off-hand way the programming has slipped in an important concept.

What if the student reacted to the ambiguous programming by writing anything but a Direct Analogy? The program tells him he has "JUST MADE A DIRECT ANALOGY." So what does he do? He looks back to admire the glittering spawn of his mind and whatever he sees there he labels "DIRECT ANALOGY."

HERE ARE SOME EXAMPLES OF DIRECT ANALOGY:
1. THE LAWN IS LIKE A RUG BECAUSE IT LOOKS LIKE A GREEN RUG.
2. THE LAWN IS LIKE A LAYER OF SKIN BECAUSE IT COVERS THE EARTH AND ACTS AS A TRANSITION ZONE BETWEEN WHAT'S ABOVE IT AND WHAT'S BELOW.
3. THE LAWN IS LIKE THE NEW YORK STOCK EXCHANGE BECAUSE IT IS AN IN-TRICATE SYSTEM WHICH DEPENDS FOR ITS EXISTANCE ON A WHOLE SERIES OF COOPERATING AND COMPETING FORCES.

THERE IS NOTHING VERY EXCITING ABOUT THE FIRST DIRECT ANALOGY — IT IS AN OBVIOUS

COMPARISON. THE SECOND DIRECT ANALOGY
MAKES YOU THINK HARDER THAN THE FIRST
ONE DOES. THAT'S BECAUSE IT'S STRANGER.
THE THIRD DIRECT ANALOGY IS THE STRANG-
EST — IT IS THE LEAST EXPECTED. YOU LEARN
THE MOST FROM A VERY STRANGE DIRECT AN-
ALOGY.

The Unit says, "YOU LEARN THE MOST FROM A VERY STRANGE
DIRECT ANALOGY." It is possible that the statement is true, but the odds
are against it. The learning process is one of reducing distance between
the learner and what is to be learned. When a student tries to make the
strange familiar and fit this strange thing into his prior experience, he
blocks learning. To the degree that an analogy is strange to a student, he
finds it difficult to make a connection that results in learning.

Furthermore, what is the student supposed to be learning anyway?
Again, the programming keeps him in the dark.

NOW TRY THE FOLLOWING PRACTICE
EXERCISES. REALLY MAKE THINGS STRANGE!

WHAT ANIMAL REMINDS YOU OF A MONKEY?

_____a. Gorilla_____

WHY?_he looks like a_____

_____monkey_____

_____

_____

_____

A "monkey" <u>is</u> an animal. There is no metaphorical content here at all. The real danger lies in students drawing the conclusion that it must be metaphorical or the item wouldn't be in the Unit.

WHAT COLOR IS ANGER? <u>Red</u>

WHY? <u>Bullfighters use red to make the bulls angry</u>

WHAT PIECE OF FURNITURE IS A MOTHER?

<u>the stove</u>

EXPLAIN YOUR CONNECTION: <u>My mother uses the stove more than anything else.</u>

The "color" item should follow the "furniture" item because there will be more "stretch" in it for most students. Try responding yourself to see which you find requires the greater imaginative leap.

By now, the student has been encouraged to respond so non-metaphorically by his first effort that he is on the wrong track and he is likely to continue to make non-metaphorical responses. The last two items would evoke a student to make a metaphorical response if the student knew how to make Direct Analogies. Therefore, the questions are not so much at fault as the context in which they are presented.

> NOW GO BACK AND IMAGINE THAT YOU
> ARE THE INSECT YOU PICKED TO BE COURAGE.
> PUT YOURSELF IN ITS PLACE. IMAGINE WHERE
> HE LIVES, WHAT HE IS UP AGAINST. BECOME
> HIM, SPEAK FOR HIM. YOU ARE THE INSECT.
> YOU ARE IN A SITUATION THAT CALLS FOR
> COURAGE! WHAT IS THAT SITUATION? HOW
> DO YOU SHOW YOUR COURAGE?

I am your ant. I'm in the army and I eat anything. I eat hamburgers and cokes and cake. I need courage to eat all that stuff!

> YOU HAVE JUST MADE A PERSONAL AN-
> ALOGY: THE IDENTIFICATION OF YOURSELF
> WITH SOMETHING OTHER THAN YOURSELF. IN
> FANTASY YOU HAVE BECOME SOMETHING ELSE.

It does not help the student to tell him after the fact that he has "JUST MADE A PERSONAL ANALOGY." In the first place, what if he hasn't? In the second place, the teacher/author's habit of explaining things after the student has responded tends to imply that there are right and wrong ways for the student to respond.

The Unit never clarifies its goals. Is it any wonder that the programming is confused? The goal might be to get insight into courage or into Direct Analogy or into Personal Analogy. At the very beginning the Unit should have established exactly what the goal was. Thus, students would have been let in on the secret. The teacher/author's choice of subject matter is his own business. Since we are discussing process here, however, it is our responsibility to be critical.

It is impossible to establish general hard and fast rules for writing an open-ended, programmed Unit because each element depends on the goals of the Unit and the context in which that element is places. It is possible, however, to point out six cardinal 'sins'.

1. THE "UN-WRITTEN" INSTRUCTION — Here the Unit assumes the student will behave in a particular way; but the student can't read the teacher/author's mind and there is no guarantee that he will behave that way.

2. "KNOWING" WHAT THE STUDENT WROTE — Here the Unit spouts an opinion about the student's effort without knowing what the student will write.

3. THE UNIMPORTANT DETAIL — The goal of the Unit is lost. There's more emphasis on the facts of the subject matter than on the connection-making process by which the student is trying to understand these facts.

4. THE FALSE EVOCATIVE QUESTION — A question can appear to be evocative, and yet lead the student to an answer that is the "right" one. Evocative questions are false when they lead to a very limited number of answers or when the wording of the question stresses one aspect so heavily that the student is blocked from making his own connection.

> 5. <u>PUTTING THOUGHTS INTO THE STUDENT'S MIND</u> — Although a Unit may be open-ended it can destroy that openness by imposing its own view on the student's efforts.
>
> 6. <u>KEEPING THE STUDENT IN THE DARK</u> — There is a particular reason for the Unit being constructed as it is, but this 'logic' is left to be discovered by the student. The standard rationalization for this method of presentation is to hail the virtue of wanting the student to "discover for himself." Th result is the student feels he is being manipulated.

COMBINING SYNECTICS WITH OTHER MODELS OF TEACHING

Unlike Nondirective Teaching, a model that easily incorporates all other models of teaching while remaining central, Synectics is a model that is most useful when *blended* with other models. The most useful features of Synectics are its techniques designed to spark creativity. These techniques should be used with the Information Processing Models. The personal-growth features of Synectics are compatible with the exploration of problems that occurs in the social models. The use of metaphoric comparisons is easily adapted to other forms of personal exploration in Simulation and Role Playing.

NONDIRECTIVE
MODEL

SCENARIO FOR THE NONDIRECTIVE MODEL

We are in a high school in suburban Chicago. John Denbro is a twenty-six-year-old English teacher who is very much concerned about Mary Ann Fortnay, one of his students. Mary Ann is a compulsive worker who does an excellent job with literature assignments and who writes excellent short stories. She is, however, reluctant to share those stories with other members of the class and declines to participate in any activities in the performing arts.

Denbro wants Mary Ann to understand why she is reluctant to allow any public display of her talents. He recognizes that the issue cannot be forced, but that he can try to help her understand why she feels the way she does. She will make her own decisions about participation that involves a sharing of her ideas.

One afternoon she comes to him with three poems she has written. She wants him to read them and give her his opinion.

Mary Ann: Mr. Denbro, could you take a look at these for me?

Denbro: Why sure, Mary Ann. Is this another short story?

Mary Ann: No, these are some poems I've been working on. I don't think they're very good, but I'd like you to tell me what you think.

103

Denbro:	When did you write them?
Mary Ann:	One Sunday afternoon a couple of weeks ago.
Denbro:	Do you remember what started you thinking that you wanted to write a poem?
Mary Ann:	I was feeling kind of sad and I remembered last month when we tried to read *The Waste Land*,[1] and it seemed to be trying to say a lot of things that we couldn't say in the usual way. I liked the beginning lines, "April is the cruelest month, breeding lilacs, lilacs out of the dead land." And that was kind of the way I felt.
Denbro:	And is this what you wrote down?
Mary Ann:	Yes. It's the first time I've ever tried writing anything like this.
Denbro:	(*reads for a few minutes and then looks up*) Mary Ann, these are really good.
Mary Ann:	What makes a poem good, Mr. Denbro?
Denbro:	Well, there are a variety of criteria for judging poetry. Some of these are technical and have to do with the quality of expression and the way one uses metaphors and analogies and other literary devices. Others are subjective and involve the quality of expression, the real beauty of the words themselves.
Mary Ann:	I felt very good when I was writing them, but when I read them over, they sound a little dumb to me.
Denbro:	What do you mean?

(At this point Denbro realizes that he may have an opportunity to explore Mary Ann's feelings about writing and help her come to grips with the ideas that she expresses.)

Mary Ann:	Oh, I don't know. I guess the main thing is that I feel ashamed if anybody else sees them.
Denbro:	Ashamed?
Mary Ann:	I really don't know. I just know that if these were to be read aloud, say to my class, I would die of mortification.
Denbro:	But you're not afraid to show them to me?
Mary Ann:	Oh no. I really trust you not to laugh or think they're funny. I thought you'd like them, even though I wasn't so sure anyone else would.
Denbro:	You really feel that the class would laugh at these?
Mary Ann:	Oh sure, they wouldn't understand.
Denbro:	How about your short stories? How do you feel about them?
Mary Ann:	You know how I feel about that. I don't want *anybody* to see what I write.

[1] T. S. Eliot, "The Waste Land," in *Collected Poems 1909-1962*. Reprinted by permission of the publishers, Harcourt Brace Jovanovich, Inc.

Denbro:	You really feel that you want to put them away somewhere so nobody can see them?
Mary Ann:	Yes, I really think so. I don't exactly know why, but I'm pretty sure that no one in my class would understand them.
Denbro:	Can you think of anybody else that might understand them?
Mary Ann:	I don't know. I kind of think there are people out there who might, but nobody around here, probably.
Denbro:	How about your parents?
Mary Ann:	Oh, they like everything I write.
Denbro:	Well, that makes three of us. Can you think of anybody else?
Mary Ann:	I guess I think adults would, but I'm not really so sure about other kids.
Denbro:	Kids are somehow different from adults in this respect.
Mary Ann:	Well, kids just don't seem to be interested in these kinds of things. I think they "put down" anybody who tries to write anything.
Denbro:	Do you think they feel that way about the authors we read in English class?
Mary Ann:	Well sometimes they do, but I guess a lot of the time they really enjoy the stories.
Denbro:	Well then, why do you think they wouldn't like what you write?
Mary Ann:	I guess I really don't know, Mr. Denbro. I guess I'm really afraid, but I can't put my finger on it.
Denbro:	Something holds you back.
Mary Ann:	In a lot of ways, I really would like to find out whether anybody really would appreciate what I write. I just don't know how to go about it.
Denbro:	How would you feel if I were to read one of your short stories but not tell them who wrote it?
Mary Ann:	Would you promise?
Denbro:	Of course I would. Then we could talk about how everybody reacted. You would know that they didn't know who had written it.
Mary Ann:	I don't know, but it sounds interesting.
Denbro:	Depending upon what happened, we could cook up some kind of strategy about what to do next.
Mary Ann:	Well, I guess you've got me right where I don't have anything to lose.
Denbro:	I hope we're always where you don't have anything to lose, Mary Ann; but there's always a risk in telling about ourselves.
Mary Ann:	What do you mean, telling about ourselves?
Denbro:	I think I should go now—but let me pick one of your stories and read

it next week, and then let's get together on Wednesday and talk about what happened.

Mary Ann: OK, and you promise not to tell?

Denbro: I promise. I'll see you next Wednesday after school.

Mary Ann: OK. Thanks a lot, Mr. Denbro. Have a good weekend.

OUTLINE OF ACTIVITIES FOR THE NONDIRECTIVE MODEL

Objectives	Materials	Activity

COMPONENT I: DESCRIBING AND UNDERSTANDING THE MODEL

Objectives	Materials	Activity
1. To realize the goals, assumptions, and procedures of the Nondirective Model.	Theory and Overview	Reading
2. To gain a sense of the model in action.	Theory in Practice	Reading
3. To recognize and use Nondirective techniques.	Taking Theory Into Action	Reading/Work with a Partner
4. To evaluate your understanding of the Nondirective Model.	Theory Checkup	Writing

COMPONENT II: VIEWING THE MODEL

Objectives	Materials	Activity
1. To become familiar with the Teaching Analysis Guide and identify items in it that you do not understand.	Teaching Analysis Guide	Reading
2. To identify phases of the model and comment on the lesson.	Demonstration Transcript	Reading/Writing/Discussion
Optional: To analyze other demonstration lessons using the Teaching Analysis Guide.	Live demonstration, audio-filmstrip, or televised lesson/Teaching Analysis Guide	Viewing/Group or Individual Analysis

COMPONENT III: PLANNING AND PEER TEACHING

Objectives	Materials	Activity
1. To select a topic for a Nondirective interview situation.	Choosing a Topic	Reading/Writing/Discussion with Partner
2. To determine behavioral objectives for the peer teaching lesson.	Determining Educational Objectives	Reading/Writing/Discussion with Partner
3. To complete the Planning Guide.	Planning Guide	Reading/Writing
4. To peer teach using the Nondirective interview strategy	Three or four peers or a student	Teaching
5. To analyze the Nondirective teaching strategy using the Teaching Analysis Guide.	Teaching Analysis Guide/Tape recorder	Writing/Listening to tape/Discussion with Partner
6. **Optional:** To use the Nondirective strategy with a student.	A student/Tape recorder	Interview
7. To analyze student lesson.	Teaching Analysis Guide	By self or with group, listen to tape recording and analyze Nondirective Interview

OUTLINE OF ACTIVITIES FOR THE NONDIRECTIVE MODEL

COMPONENT IV: ADAPTING THE MODEL

1. To present the Nondirective strategy for the whole classroom.

   Curriculum Possibilities and Adaptations

   Reading

2. To plan the use of the Nondirective strategy for long-term development of student-centered learning.

   Long-term Plans

   Reading

3. To be aware of the possibilities of combining the Nondirective strategy with other models of teaching.

   Combining the Nondirective Strategy with Other Models

   Reading

Component I

DESCRIBING
AND UNDERSTANDING
THE MODEL

THEORY AND OVERVIEW

The Nondirective Model of teaching and the Synectics Model both focus on personal growth in students. Although these models are appropriate for cognitive learning, they involve students in more than an acquisition of facts, for they both emphasize affective development in students. The Nondirective Model and Synectics stress skills that you can use in working with students in a variety of classroom settings—the whole class, groups of students, or an individual student. As a family of teaching models, Synectics and Nondirective Teaching emphasize the unique development of individual students.

The Nondirective Model is based on the work of Carl Rogers and other advocates of nondirective counseling. Rogers extends his view of therapy as a mode of learning to education. For Rogers, positive human relationships enable people to grow, and, therefore, the organization of instruction should be drawn from concepts of human relations rather than from a concept of subject matter, thought processes, or other intellectual sources. Developing Rogers' ideas, we see the teacher's role in Nondirective Teaching as that of a facilitator who has a personal relationship with students in guiding their growth and development.

The Nondirective Model asserts that the role of the teacher should be to facilitate selection in learning. In this role, the teacher helps students explore new ideas about their lives, their schoolwork, and their relations with others. The model assumes that students are willing to be responsible for their own learning. The teacher facilitates learning in individual or group work by using such techniques as contracting projects and special assignments in resource centers.

The Nondirective Teaching Model can be used in a classroom learning environment as well as for group or individual counseling. In any approach to the model, the expansion of learning depends on the willingness of student and teacher to share ideas openly and to communicate honestly with one another. The personal family of models of teaching describes learning environments that hope to nurture students rather than control student learning. These models are more concerned with long-term learning styles and with developing individual personalities than they are with short-term instructional or content objectives.

This system for studying Nondirective Teaching consists of four components. As you decide upon the component to begin with, think about your own learning style. You may or may not want to approach this model as you approach others in the series. As with Synectics, interaction with group members is important; some of the exercises ask you to work with a partner. Sharing your impressions of the nondirective style with other teachers enhances the personal growth features of this model.

Goals of Nondirective Teaching

The Nondirective Model focuses on facilitating learning. The primary goal of Nondirective Teaching is to assist students as they reorganize their inner selves for greater personal integration, effectiveness, and realistic self-appraisal. The secondary goal is to create a learning environment conducive to the process of stimulating, examining, and evaluating new perceptions. The students assume responsibility for the direction of their own learning. The teacher withdraws from directive decision-making modes and concentrates on facilitating learning styles. Crucial to the process is a reexamination of needs and values—their sources and outcomes. Students do not necessarily need to change, but the goal of the teacher is to help students understand their own needs and values so that they can direct their own educational decisions.

Assumptions About Nondirective Teaching

The Nondirective Model draws on concepts developed by Carl Rogers for nondirective counseling. In this kind of counseling, the client's capacity to deal constructively with his own life is respected. Similarly, in Nondirective Teaching the teacher respects the students' ability to identify their own problems and to formulate solutions.

The Nondirective Model assumes that the student can be part of the decision-making process for learning. Nondirective Teaching is student-centered. The facilitator sees the world as the student sees it. This creates an atmosphere of empathetic communication in which the student's self-direction can be nurtured and developed.

The teacher facilitates student self-direction through the nondirective interview strategy. Through this technique, the teacher mirrors students' thoughts and feelings. By using reflecting strategies, the teacher raises the students' consciousness of their perceptions and feelings as they relate to classroom learning, personal problems, or individual concerns. This technique helps students clarify their ideas.

A second function of the teacher is to serve as a benevolent alter ego, one who accepts all feelings and thoughts, even those the students may be afraid of or may view as wrong, or perhaps even punishable. In being accepting and nonpunitive, the teacher indirectly communicates to the students that all thoughts and feelings are acceptable. In fact, recognition of both positive and negative feelings is essential to emotional development and positive solutions. The model assumes that students are able and willing, with assistance from the teacher, to function in a learning environment where decisions about what is important in school are made by students, alone or jointly with the teacher.

In Nondirective Teaching, the teacher serves as a facilitator—helping students deal with a range of academic, social, and personal problems. The facilitative counseling style is one of many approaches to helping students cope with their problems. Other approaches, though useful, do not result in the strengthened understanding and knowledge of oneself and others that develops within the security of an empathetic relationship.

The Nondirective Interview

The main technique for developing facilitative relationships is the nondirective interview, a series of face-to-face encounters between teacher and student. During the interview, the teacher serves as a collaborator in the process of student self-exploration and problem solving. The interview itself is designed to focus on the uniqueness of the individual and the importance of emotional life in all human activity. Nondirective Teaching's use of the interview technique is borrowed from counseling, but the technique is not the same in the classroom as it is in the clinical setting.

Within the classroom, the interview is used as a learning experience, but its content is not confined solely to personal problems—a much more common focus of counseling. A teacher using the nondirective interview strategy can counsel students about class-assignment progress, evaluate the progress of individual students in their work, and help students to explore new topics that may be of interest to them. Although the Nondirective strategy is appropriate for dealing with students who are having personal problems or problems in school, it is equally appropriate to use the technique with students who are successful in school and not having personal problems. Nondirective interview techniques help students strengthen their self-perceptions and evaluate their individual progress and development in learning situations.

The nondirective interview technique is similar whether it is used for academic counseling, behavioral counseling, or a combination of the two. The teacher gives up the traditional authoritarian decision-making role, choosing instead the role of a facilitator who focuses on student feelings. Also, the teacher as counselor is not an advisor. The relationship between student and teacher in a nondirective interview is best described as a *partnership*. Thus, if the student complains of poor grades and an inability to study, the teacher as facilitator does not attempt to resolve the problem simply by explaining the art of good study habits. Instead, the teacher encourages the student to express those feelings about school, himself, and other persons that may surround his inability to concentrate. When these feelings are fully explored and perceptions are clarified, the student himself tries to identify appropriate changes and bring them about.

According to Rogers, the best interview atmosphere has four definite qualities. First, the teacher shows warmth and responsiveness, expressing genuine interest in the student and accepting him as a person. These attributes are manifested in a special kind of dialogue. Second, the counseling relationship is characterized by permissiveness in regard to the expression of feeling. The teacher does not judge or moralize. Because of the importance of emotions, much content is discussed that would normally be guarded against in more customary student relationships with teachers or advisors. Third, the student is free to express symbolically his feelings, but he is not free to control the teacher or to carry impulses into action. In the counseling situation, there are definite limitations in terms of responsibility, time, affection, and aggressive action. Fourth, the counseling relationship is free from any type of pressure or coercion. The teacher avoids showing personal bias or reacting in a personally critical manner to the student during the interview session.

In the nondirective interview, the teacher wants the student to pass through three stages of personal growth: (1) a release of feelings, (2) insight followed by action, and (3) integration that leads to a new orientation. Figure 1 illustrates this process.

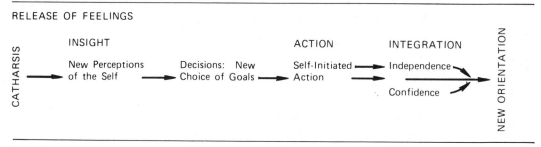

Figure 1. *Phases of Personal Growth in the Nondirective Interview Process.*

The teacher depends on three concepts for assessing the direction and progress of the counseling process that takes place in the nondirective interview: (1) release of feeling (or catharsis), (2) insight, and (3) integration. These concepts are interrelated in the process of nondirective counseling in that they all stress the feeling or emotional elements of the situation. Each concept functions separately, but unity of the three is essential for a successful counseling experience. The use of these concepts is equally important in counseling for classroom problems and for personal problems.

The *release of feelings (catharsis)* involves the breaking down of the emotional barriers that often impair a person's ability to solve dilemmas. By discharging the emotions surrounding a problem, a person paves the way for developing a new perspective or insight into the problem. Usually, people are not conscious of these emotional barriers. They may be dimly aware of them, but often they are afraid to search for, express, and acknowledge emotional barriers. The function of catharsis in nondirective counseling is to bring feelings to the fore in order that more constructive emotional attitudes may emerge, attitudes that facilitate decision-making, new behaviors, and new actions.

According to Rogers, responding on an intellectual basis to students' problems inhibits the expression of feelings, which are, after all, at the root of the problem. Without the release and exploration of these feelings, students will reject suggestions and be unable to sustain real behavior changes. On the other hand, catharsis, with its therapeutic effects, permits a solid "working through" of a problem.

Catharsis initiates the problem-solving process as follows: At first, a person has pent-up feelings. He is tense, defensive, and, as a result, is unable to see his problem and himself clearly. The student-centered counseling situation presents an opportunity for free personal expression. The student becomes less tense as he experiences the release that comes with the expression of pent-up feelings. Free of these feelings, the student is more comfortable and explores more aspects of himself. Gradually, he becomes aware of and accepts all sides of himself—his strengths as well as his weaknesses.

Insight is the short-term goal of the cathartic process. A student involved in nondirective counseling experiences more than the release of feelings. He experiences the insight that leads to a reorganization of the self and to increased understanding of one's emotions and patterns of behavior. Indications of insight come from statements by the student that describe behavior in terms of cause and effect, or in terms of personal meaning. As the student begins to understand the reasons for his behaviors, he begins to see other, more functional ways of satisfying his needs. Through the release of emotions, the student can perceive his options more clearly. New insights enable the student to select delayed goals that are more satisfying over goals that give immediate but only temporary satisfaction.

Ultimately, the test of personal insight is the presence of actions that motivate the student toward new goals. At first, these positive actions may concern minor issues, but they create a sense of confidence and independence in the student. Gradually, the student's positive action, at first sporadic and disparate in its focus, begins to accumulate around a single problem area, thereby leading to a new, more comprehensive orientation. We can think of this phase as *integration*, the long-term goal of the nondirective interview.

These three phases of the nondirective interview—catharsis, insight, and integration—are the same for counseling with an individual or with a small group. During any interview, the facilitator works toward these three goals. In school use of the counseling relationship, the nondirective interview is a technique by which teachers can help students focus the direction of their own learning. In accomplishing this end, the teacher may consider personal problems, but the model does not deal exclusively with such problems and is not intended to supplant counseling from other sources.

The nondirective approach maintains that the most effective means of uncovering the emotions underlying a problem is to follow the pattern of the students' feelings as they are freely expressed. Instead of asking direct questions for the purpose of eliciting feelings, the teacher lets the students direct the flow of thoughts and feelings. If the students express themselves freely, the problem and its underlying emotions will emerge. This process is facilitated by reflecting the students' feelings, thereby bringing them into awareness and sharper focus.

A number of specific skills are used by teachers to facilitate the nondirective strategy. The most basic of these skills is the ability to perceive and reflect the feelings of the student. This is a difficult skill for most of us because we are more attuned to the content of what people are saying than to their emotional attitudes. Unlike other kinds of teacher-student relationships, nondirective counseling focuses on the emotional element of the students' behavior. The nondirective strategy usually looks to three sources of student problems: (1) present feelings, (2) distorted perceptions, and (3) alternatives that are unexplored because of an emotional reaction to them. Elimination of these difficulties is brought about not by direct solutions (deciding what to do), but by getting rid of negative feelings and distorted perceptions (dealing with the emotional content of decision making and thought processes).

We have identified four general categories of techniques that are appropriate for nondirective interviews:

1. nondirective lead-taking
2. nondirective responses to feeling
3. semidirective responses to feeling
4. directive counseling moves

Each of these types of responses is intended to maintain the nondirective dimension of the counseling by stressing the sharing of responsibility equally between teacher and student for decision making. These techniques (to be described in Taking Theory Into Action) are also designed to promote the release of feeling, insight, and integration. Although the focus of the nondirective interview allows the student freedom to identify and explore problems, the teacher will at times have to employ directive counseling moves in order to help the student. These moves are used infrequently and only if a student is unable to focus or limit his concerns.

The nondirective interview strategy may be used for several types of problem situations: personal, social, and academic. In the case of a personal problem, the individual explores his feelings about himself. In social problems, he explores his feelings about his relationships with others and investigates how his feelings about himself may influence these relationships. In an academic problem, he explores his feelings about his competence and interests. In each case, however, the interview content is always personal rather than external; it centers on the individual's own feelings, experiences, insights, and solutions.

Although one-to-one interviews may arise spontaneously at the student's initiation, this training system, because its objective is teacher training, can only account for those encounters that are initiated by the teacher. However, regardless of who the initiator is, the basic strategy should remain the same.

Syntax of the Nondirective Teaching Strategy

Putting the nondirective stance into operation presents some interesting problems. First, the responsibility for the initiation and maintenance of the interview is largely in the hands of the student. In most models of teaching, the teacher actively shapes events and can picture the pattern of activities that lie ahead; but in most counseling situations, events emerge and the pattern of activities is fluid. Little is consciously controlled by either student or teacher. Second, from the teacher's point of view counseling is made up of a series of response moves. These moves occur in no predictable sequence. This is unlike most teacher-controlled teaching strategies, where the activities are broad and sequential yet distinct from one another, as in presenting information and then analyzing it. As teaching becomes more student-centered, it becomes less a sequence of activities and more a series of principles for reacting that the teachers use to guide their response to the needs of the situation.

Since Nondirective Teaching assumes that every student, every situation, and every teacher is unique, the events in a nondirective interview situation cannot be anticipated. To master Nondirective Teaching, teachers learn general principles, work to increase their sensitivity to others, master the nondirective skills, and then practice making contact with students and responding to them, using skills drawn from a repertoire of nondirective counseling techniques.

Despite the fluidity and unpredictability of the nondirective strategy, Rogers points out that the nondirective interview has a sequence. We have divided this sequence into five phases of activity, as shown in Figure 2.

Phase One. In Phase One, the helping situation is defined. This includes structuring remarks by the counselor that define the student's freedom to express feelings, an agreement on the general focus of the interview, an initial problem statement, some discussion of the relationship if it is to be ongoing, and the establishment of procedures for meeting. Phase One generally occurs during the initial interview in an ongoing relationship; however, some structuring or definition by the teacher may be necessary for some time, even if this consists only of occasional summarizing moves that redefine the problem and reflect progress. Naturally, these structuring and definitional comments vary considerably with the type of interview, the specific problem, and the student. Negotiating academic contracts will likely differ from working with behavioral problem situations. Voluntary and involuntary counseling situations are likely to be shaped differently. (Academic contracts will be discussed in greater detail in Component IV.)

Phase One: Helping Situation is Defined	Phase Two: Encouraging Exploration of the Problem	Phase Three: Developing Insight
Teacher encourages free expression of feeling.	Individual expresses negative feelings. Teacher accepts and clarifies negative feelings.	
Phase Four: Planning and Decision-Making	*Action Outside the Interview* Student initiates positive actions.	**Phase Five: Integration**
Teacher clarifies possible decisions.		Student gains further insight and develops more positive actions.

Figure 2. *Sequence of the Nondirective Interview.*

Phase Two: The student is encouraged, by the teacher's acceptance and clarification, to express negative and positive feelings, to state and explore the problem.

Phase Three. Gradually, the student develops insight: he perceives new meaning in his experience, sees new relationships of cause and effect, and understands the meaning of his previous behavior. In most situations, it seems that the student alternates between exploration of the problem itself and the development of new insight into his feelings. Both of these are necessary for progress. Discussion of the problem without exploration of feelings would indicate that the student himself—his own feelings—was being avoided.

Phase Four. The student moves toward planning and decision-making with respect to the problem. The role of the teacher is to clarify the alternatives.

Phase Five. The student reports the actions he has taken, develops further insight, and plans increasingly more integrated and positive actions.

The syntax presented here could occur in one interview or a series of interviews. In the latter case, Phases One and Two could occur in the first few interviews, Phases Three and Four in the next, and Phase Five in the last interview. Or, if the interview consisted of a voluntary meeting with a student who had an immediate problem, Phases One through Four could occur in the one meeting, with the student returning briefly to report his actions and insights. On the other hand, the interviews involved in negotiating academic contracts are sustained for a period of time, and the context of each meeting generally involves some kind of planning and decision-making, although several interviews devoted entirely to exploring a problem might occur.

The five phases of the nondirective interview provide the teacher with an overview of the process being engaged in, though the specific flow is only minimally in the teacher's control. The syntax varies with different functions, problems, and personalities.

Social System

The social system of the Nondirective strategy has little external structure. It requires the teacher to assume the roles of facilitator and reflector. The student is primarily responsible for the initiation and maintenance of the interaction process (control); authority is shared between student and teacher. The norms are those of open expression of feelings and autonomy of thought and behavior. Rewards, in the usual sense of approval of specific behavior—and particularly punishment—do not apply in this strategy. The rewards in a nondirective interview are more subtle and intrinsic—acceptance, understanding, and empathy from the teacher. The knowledge of oneself and the psychological rewards gained from self-reliance are generated by the student himself.

Principles of Reaction

The principles of reaction for the teacher are based on nondirective responses and on the avoidance of responses that characterize a more directive stance. These principles are really the essence of the strategy. The teacher reaches out to the student, "feels" his personality and his problems, and reacts in such a way as to help the student define his problems and feelings, take responsibility for his actions, and plan his objectives and how to achieve them.

Support System

The support system for this strategy varies with the function of the interview. If the interview is for the purpose of negotiating academic contracts, then the necessary resources have to be available for the student to carry out the self-directed learning in a learning center of some kind. If the interview consists of counseling for a behavioral problem, no resources beyond the skills of the teacher are necessary. In both cases, the one-to-one situation requires spatial arrangements that allow for privacy, removal from other classroom forces and activities, and time to explore a problem adequately and in an unhurried fashion.

SUMMARY CHART: NONDIRECTIVE MODEL

Syntax

> Phase One: Helping situation is defined
> Teacher encourages free expression of feeling.
>
> Phase Two: Exploration of the problem
> Student is encouraged to define problem.
> Teacher accepts and clarifies feelings.
>
> Phase Three: Developing insights
> Student discusses problem.
> Teacher supports student.
>
> Phase Four: Planning and decision-making
> Student plans initial decision-making.
> Teacher clarifies possible decisions.
>
> Phase Five: Integration
> Student gains further insight and makes more positive decisions.
> Teacher is supportive.

Principles of Reaction

> Teacher reaches out to student, empathizes with student, reacts to help student define problem and take action to achieve a solution.

Social System

> Little external structure. Teacher facilitates; student initiates problem-centered discussion. Rewards, in the usual sense of approval of specific behavior, and particularly punishment, do not apply in this strategy. The rewards are intrinsic and include acceptance, empathy, and understanding from the teacher.

Support System

> Teacher needs quiet, private place for one-to-one contacts, resource center for conferences on academic contracts.

THEORY IN PRACTICE

No amount of description can convey a sense of a model of teaching as well as an example of the model in practice. In fact, reading too much theory before gaining a rough "image" of the practice can be confusing and, for some people, frustrating and discouraging. So we encourage you, at this point of your study of the Nondirective Teaching Model, to read the following abbreviated transcript of an actual classroom session. We suggest that you first read only the teacher-student dialogue and then go back to note the annotations. Remember, the goal at this point in your training is to gain a sense of the model—its flow and feeling—not to master the techniques of implementation.

In this transcript, the teacher and the student use the nondirective interview to explore the student's communication difficulties with her parents. Through structuring and questioning techniques, the teacher helps the student explore her perceptions of her parents. At the conclusion of the interview nothing has been resolved, but the student wants to try to view her parents from a new perspective.

T: VERONICA, YOU WERE MENTIONING EARLIER SOMETHING THAT WAS BOTHERING YOU, AND I THOUGHT WE COULD TAKE THIS OPPORTUNITY TO LOOK AT THAT PROBLEM. I CAN'T SOLVE IT FOR YOU, BUT I THOUGHT THAT MAYBE BY TALKING ABOUT IT WITH SOMEBODY, YOU MIGHT BE ABLE TO SEE IT DIFFERENTLY. I'D LIKE YOU TO TELL ME A LITTLE BIT MORE ABOUT IT; I'M NOT CLEAR HOW YOU SAW THE PROBLEM.

Phase One: Helping Situation Is Defined

Structuring

S: OK. I FELT THAT THE YOUNGER GENERATION WAS BEING IGNORED BY THOSE OLDER THAN US. USUALLY, THOSE OLDER THAN US FEEL THAT WE HAVE NOT LIVED ENOUGH TO KNOW AS THEY DO, BUT I FEEL THAT TIMES HAVE CHANGED. A LOT OF THINGS HAVE HAPPENED BETWEEN THEIR YEARS AND OUR YEARS, AND PERHAPS THEY CAN SEE OUR WAY DIFFERENTLY. IT'S NOT THAT WE JUST WANT TO SPEAK OUT, YOU KNOW, 'CAUSE WE JUST FEEL LIKE IT, YOU KNOW, JUST TO GET RIGHTS OR ANYTHING; IT'S JUST THAT WE WANT TO EXPRESS OUR OPINIONS. MOST LIKELY WE'LL BE IGNORED.

T: LET ME SEE IF I UNDERSTAND THIS. YOU THINK THAT PEOPLE WHO ARE OLDER THAN YOU ARE NOT PAYING ATTENTION TO YOUR OPINIONS.

Phase Two: Encouraging Exploration of the Problem Content

S: UH-HUH.

T: BECAUSE THEY'VE LIVED LONGER AND THERE-FORE THEY BELIEVE YOU DON'T REALLY KNOW WHAT YOU'RE SAYING BECAUSE YOU HAVEN'T LIVED AS LONG.

Paraphrase content

S: UH-HUH.

T: DID YOU SAY THAT PEOPLE YOUNGER THAN YOU ARE NOT LISTENING TO YOU?

Direct question

S: OLDER.

T: OK, IT'S JUST THE OLDER ONES. YOU'VE PUT THAT IN A VERY GENERAL TERM. HAS THIS HAP-PENED TO YOU IN A SPECIFIC INCIDENT?

Probing with another direct question

S: WELL, FOR ONE THING, I'M SECOND TO THE YOUNGEST, AND I'VE HAD FIVE SISTERS OLDER THAN ME. I HAVE FIVE OLDER SISTERS. AND WE'VE ALL GONE THROUGH A STAGE, OK? USUALLY WE DO WHAT EVERYBODY HAS HAD THE OPPORTUNITY TO DO, BUT WE CANNOT DO WHAT THEY COULD NOT DO. I FEEL THAT IT SHOULDN'T BE JUST BECAUSE ONE PERSON WASN'T ABLE TO DO SOMETHING, YOU AREN'T ABLE TO DO IT ALSO, BECAUSE, YOU KNOW, WE ARE ALL DIFFERENT.

T: IS THERE SOMETHING SPECIFIC YOU WOULD LIKE TO DO THAT YOUR SISTERS HAVEN'T?   Direct question

S: IN MY FAMILY, MY PARENTS AREN'T EXACTLY STRICT. THEY JUST HAVE CERTAIN RULES, AND, WELL, MY OLDER SISTERS HAVE BEEN A LITTLE MORE SHY THAN I AM.

T: SHY?   Minimal encouragement

S: YEAH, YOU KNOW. THEY DON'T SPEAK AS MUCH AS I DO, AND I LIKE TO TALK A LOT, AND I LIKE TO DO MORE THINGS, AND I HAVE DIFFERENT IDEAS THAN THEY DO. LIKE I SAY, I AM ONLY ABLE TO DO WHAT THEY DO. AND—I DON'T KNOW—I JUST WANT TO GET OUT MORE.

T: YOU WANT TO GET OUT MORE?   Minimal encouragement

S: YEAH, I DON'T KNOW, I GUESS IT'S—WHAT I FEEL IS LIKE I'M TRYING TO BE OLDER THAN WHAT I AM, TRYING TO GROW TOO FAST.

T: YOU FEEL THAT?

S: NO, THAT'S WHAT THEY FEEL. PERHAPS IT MIGHT BE. I GUESS I DO WANT TO GET OLD FAST—BUT I DON'T THINK THAT'S RIGHT EITHER. I DON'T KNOW, I JUST WANT TO BE ABLE TO DO THINGS, NOT JUST DO IT LIKE ANOTHER PERSON'S LIFE.

T: CAN YOU TELL ME ONE THING THAT YOU WOULD LIKE TO DO THAT'S DIFFERENT THAN WHAT YOUR SISTERS HAVE DONE?   Directive question

S: WELL, LIKE, WE HAVE FRIENDS, OTHER GIRLS, AND, I DON'T KNOW, I LIKE TO COMMUNICATE WITH THEM A LOT. I LIKE TO COMMUNICATE WITH MY SISTERS, BUT THEY HAVE THEIR OWN PROBLEMS ALSO. SO I FEEL FREER TO TALK TO MY FRIENDS THAN I DO MY FAMILY. AND MY PARENTS, THEY FEEL THAT YOUR PROBLEMS SHOULD BE DISCUSSED WITH YOUR FAMILY MORE THAN YOUR FRIENDS, BECAUSE THEY FEEL THEY KNOW MORE ABOUT YOU THAN YOUR FRIENDS DO.

T: SO THAT'S ONE WAY YOU WOULD LIKE TO DO THINGS DIFFERENTLY THAN YOUR SISTERS HAVE DONE THEM. HOW DOES IT MAKE YOU FEEL WHEN THEY TELL YOU THAT?

S: UM, WELL, DISCOURAGED, DISAPPOINTED—THAT'S ABOUT IT.

T: HOW DO YOU HANDLE THE PROBLEM?   Open question

S: ARGUMENTS SOMETIMES, BUT THEN I FEEL IT'S JUST A WASTE OF TIME.

T: SO, YOU GET PRETTY ANGRY ABOUT IT?   Reflection of feeling

S: YEAH, BUT IT JUST SEEMS I DON'T REALLY GET ANYTHING DONE, SO SOMETIMES I JUST KEEP IT IN MYSELF.

T: WHAT DO YOU MEAN WHEN YOU SAY YOU DON'T GET ANYTHING DONE?   Direct question

S: WELL, LIKE , WHAT I'M TRYING TO DO IS GET MYSELF NOTICED AND HOW I AM. I GUESS THEY DO LISTEN, BUT I WANT TO BE ABLE TO DO WHAT I WANT TO. NOT THAT I WANT FREEDOM, EXACTLY; I JUST WANT TO BE MORE ASSOCIATED WITH PEOPLE.

T: MORE TIME WITH YOUR FRIENDS. HOW DO YOU FEEL YOUR FAMILY REACTS WHEN YOU TELL THEM THIS?   Open question

S: WHAT THEY THINK OF MOSTLY IS THE WAY THEY LOOKED AND WHAT THEY WENT THROUGH IN THEIR CHILDHOODS. THEY FEEL IT'S GOING TO HAPPEN THE SAME WAY TO ME.

T: AND HOW DO YOU RESPOND?

S: I TELL THEM THAT I'M RESPONSIBLE AND THAT I WANT TO PROVE TO THEM THAT I'M ABLE TO HANDLE MYSELF—THINGS LIKE THAT.

T: AND . . .   Minimal encouragement

S: KINDA JUST GOES OFF. I DON'T KNOW, THEY JUST SAY—WELL, THEY LISTEN, BUT LIKE I SAID, IT DOESN'T SEEM LIKE I GET ANYWHERE.

T: YOU MEAN THEY DON'T CHANGE THEIR OPINION ABOUT WHAT YOU CAN AND CAN'T DO.   Paraphrase content

S: UH-HUH.

T: DO YOU TALK TO YOUR FRIENDS, ANYWAY?   Direct question

S: WELL, AT SCHOOL; THAT'S ABOUT IT. AT HOME, I DON'T HAVE ALL MY FRIENDS OVER.

T: SO, ONE OF THE CONSEQUENCES OF THIS IS THAT YOU DON'T HAVE YOUR FRIENDS OVER BECAUSE YOU FEEL THAT YOUR PARENTS DON'T WANT YOU TO TALK TO YOUR FRIENDS—   **Phase Three: Developing Insight**

S: ABOUT PERSONAL THINGS.

T: AND THAT YOU'LL BE TOO CLOSE TO THEM?

S: OR THAT I MIGHT GET THEIR IDEAS. AND, YOU KNOW, I UNDERSTAND THAT, BUT I DON'T REALLY GET THEIR IDEAS FROM MY FRIENDS; IT'S WHAT I FEEL. SOMETIMES I FEEL THAT I GET MY IDEAS FROM MY FRIENDS.

T: YOU THINK THAT THEY FEEL THAT YOU'RE GOING TO BE INFLUENCED BY YOUR FRIENDS?   Paraphrase

S: UH-HUH.

T: AND YOU DON'T FEEL THAT YOU ARE.

S: UH-UH.

T: MUST BE PRETTY FRUSTRATING. WHAT KIND OF IDEAS DO YOUR FRIENDS HAVE?   Simple acceptance: directive question

S: WELL, MY FRIENDS DO MORE OUTGOING THINGS THAN I DO, BUT IT DOESN'T MEAN THAT—I MEAN, I GO TO FOOTBALL GAMES AND EVERYTHING LIKE THAT, BUT, LIKE, AFTERWARDS THEY GO OUT, LIKE TO A PIZZA PARLOR, OR SOMETIMES THEY GO TO THE BEACH, AND THEY STAY OUT LONGER THAN I DO. I UNDERSTAND MY PARENTS' PART; THEY FEEL LIKE THEY DO BECAUSE THEY CARE; THEY FEEL A RESPONSIBILITY FOR WHAT HAPPENS TO ME, YOU KNOW? AND, LIKE I SAID, ALL I WANT IS TO SHOW THAT I'M RESPONSIBLE AND CAN TAKE CARE OF MYSELF.

T: YOU'D LIKE TO DO THINGS LIKE STAY OUT—   Paraphrase

S: NOT TOO LATE, AS THEY DO.

T: DO YOU PRESENT THESE TO YOUR PARENTS, SPECIFICALLY, LIKE STAYING OUT AT THE PIZZA PARLOR?   Directive question

S: WELL, MY PARENTS FEEL THAT IT'S TOO ROWDY, AND IT IS SOMETIMES. BUT IT ISN'T LIKE I'M JUST THERE TO WATCH OR ANYTHING; I'M MOST LIKELY TO LEAVE THE PLACE RIGHT AWAY.

T: HAVE YOU TOLD THEM THAT?

S: YEAH.

T: AND THEY MIGHT GIVE YOU AN OPPORTUNITY—

S: — TO TRY IT, YEAH.

T: HAVE YOU ASKED THEM FOR AN OPPORTUNITY?

S: I GUESS TALKING TO THEM SHOWED I DID WANT AN OPPORTUNITY, BUT THEY JUST HAVEN'T GIVEN ME THE CHANCE. AND, LIKE I SAID, IT DOESN'T BOTHER ME—I MEAN, IT DOES BOTHER ME, BUT, LIKE, AS I'M GETTING OLDER, I MEAN, I'M JUST GROWING OUT OF IT. LIKE I SAID, THE OLDER I GET, THEY FEEL I'M GETTING MORE RESPONSIBLE, RIGHT? SO IT'S KINDA LIKE WEARING OFF.

T: WHAT'S WEARING OFF?

S: BEING RESPONSIBLE. I MEAN, THEY HAVEN'T GOT TO IT STRAIGHT, BECAUSE I'M SIXTEEN, AND MY BIRTHDAY COMES A LONG WAY, AND IT SEEMS LIKE I GROW OLDER SLOWER THAN MY OTHER SISTERS DID, AND THEY LOOK UPON ME LIKE I'M INFLUENCED BY MY FRIENDS AND LIKE I'M NOT BEING LIKE MY SISTERS.

T: YOU THINK YOU'RE GETTING FEWER PRIVILEGES THAN YOUR SISTERS DID AT THE SAME AGE.   Paraphrase content

S: YEAH, I GUESS.

T: WHEN YOU SAID, "I'M GROWING OLDER MORE SLOWLY THAN MY SISTERS," BY THAT YOU MEAN YOU'RE GETTING FEWER PRIVILEGES?

S: I GUESS I FEEL THAT WAY, YEAH.

T: I'M ALSO HEARING THAT YOUR SISTERS WERE PRETTY MUCH THE WAY YOUR PARENTS WANTED THEM TO BE, AND SOMEHOW YOU'RE DIFFERENT THAN YOUR PARENTS EXPECT YOU TO BE, AND DIFFERENT FROM YOUR SISTERS. DO YOU FEEL DIFFERENT FROM YOUR SISTERS?   Paraphrase

S: SOMETIMES. WELL, YEAH, I GUESS I AM—WE ALL ARE, IN A WAY. LIKE I SAID, I TALK MORE THAN THEY ALL DO.

T: YOU EXPRESS YOUR OPINIONS MORE?

S: UH-HUH.

T: HOW DO YOU FEEL YOUR PARENTS SEE THAT?   Open question

S: WELL, I QUIT TALKING ABOUT IT A LOT TO MY PARENTS; I JUST KEEP IT TO MYSELF MORE. BUT WHEN THEY DID HEAR ABOUT IT, THEY JUST DISAGREED WITH ME.

T: BECAUSE YOU DON'T FEEL YOU CAN GET THROUGH TO YOUR PARENTS, YOU SORT OF STOPPED TALKING TO THEM, OR MAYBE YOU HAD BEEN MORE OPEN, AND ALSO YOU STOPPED BRINGING YOUR FRIENDS HOME.   Paraphrase content

S: UH-HUH.

T: WELL, IS THIS SOMETHING YOU'D LIKE TO CHANGE?   **Phase Four: Planning/Decision Making**

S: I GUESS I WOULD. BUT LIKE I SAID, NOW IT'S PASSING BY SO FAST THAT THEY HAVE GIVEN ME THE PRIVILEGE TO HAVE FRIENDS—   Integration: student has more positive insight into the situation

T: THEY HAVE GIVEN YOU MORE PRIVILEGES.

S: YEAH, BUT NOT EXACTLY "FRIENDS" FRIENDS, YOU KNOW, TO GO OUT WITH THEM AND TO BE WITH THEM ALONE. USUALLY, IT'S JUST RIGHT AT THE HOUSE, BUT, LIKE, NOT BEING ABLE TO HAVE A WHOLE GROUP OR ANYTHING LIKE THAT.

T: SO THEY'VE GIVEN YOU PERMISSION TO HAVE A FEW PEOPLE OVER AT A TIME, BUT NOT AS MANY AS YOU'D LIKE TO HAVE?   Reflection of feeling

S: YEAH, OR GO OUT WITH THEM.

T: AND YOU CAN'T GO OUT. HOW'S THAT WORKING OUT?   Open question

S: WELL, I GOT TO THAT STAGE SO FAR, I DON'T KNOW.

T: SO YOU'RE JUST FINDING OUT. HOW DO YOU FEEL ABOUT IT?   Paraphrase

S: BETTER, I GUESS.

T: DO YOU STILL HAVE ANY NEGATIVE FEELINGS ABOUT THAT?   Direct question

S: WELL, LIKE, I'M GOING THROUGH MY LAST PART OF MY SENIOR YEAR. I MEAN I'M GOING TO BE GOING THROUGH MY SENIOR YEAR, SO, I DON'T KNOW, I GUESS I JUST HOPE FOR THE BEST. I JUST HOPE FOR THE BEST—THAT THEY FEEL THAT I'M MORE RESPONSIBLE.

T: YOU'RE NOT SURE THAT THEY DO?   Reflection of feeling

S: UH-HUH.

T: HOW DOES THAT MAKE YOU FEEL?

S: (looks down) I DON'T KNOW. SAD, I GUESS. IT DOES SOMETIMES, YEAH.

T: CAN BE UNCOMFORTABLE.   Reflection of feeling

S: YEAH.

T: LISTEN, I APPRECIATE YOUR TALKING ABOUT   Structuring: concluding the session
THIS WITH ME, AND I DON'T KNOW IF IT'S BEEN
OF HELP TO YOU, TO CLEAR THINGS UP. WE
HAVEN'T SOLVED OR CHANGED ANYTHING WITH
YOUR PARENTS, BUT MAYBE IT WAS HELPFUL TO
TALK.

TAKING THEORY INTO ACTION

This section delineates the role of the teacher as counselor in the nondirective interview strategy and outlines techniques used in the interview. Accompanying the descriptive material and the examples is a series of exercises designed to provide you with some practice. If you work with a colleague while doing these exercises, you will approximate the interview more closely than if you work alone. We urge you to work with someone because of the personal relationship that is the heart of the strategy.

Role of the Teacher in the Nondirective Interview

To effectively use the Nondirective Model, a teacher must be willing to accept that a student can understand and cope with his own life. Belief in the student's capacity to direct himself is communicated through the teacher's attitude and verbal behavior. The teacher does not attempt to judge, advise, reassure, or encourage the student. Such stances indicate limited confidence in the student's capabilities. The teacher does not attempt to diagnose problems. Instead, the teacher attempts to perceive the student's world as the student sees and feels it. And, at the moment of the student's self-perception, the teacher communicates this understanding of the student's self-perception to the student. In this model, the teacher temporarily sets aside personal thoughts and feelings and reflects the student's feelings and thoughts. By doing this, the teacher conveys deep understanding and acceptance of the student's feelings. The teacher's role in the nondirective interview is to perceive as accurately as possible the world as the student sees or experiences it, and to reflect these perceptions to the student in an accepting, nonthreatening way.

The theory behind the teacher's role in the nondirective interview is that people deny feelings that they perceive as incongruous or incompatible with their view of themselves. If we perceive ourselves as kind, sympathetic individuals, we usually repress feelings of anger or hostility, for they contradict our view of ourselves. Yet when we do this, the problems surrounding these feelings fail to be resolved and we continue to occupy a less effective state of being. What we need, the theory holds, is an alter ego who can bring these feelings into our awareness in an atmosphere of safety and acceptance.

The nondirective teacher assumes that role of alter ego. To function in such a role, the teacher needs to develop an *internal* frame of reference—to perceive as the student perceives. Expressing the student's feeling in terms of "you" rather than "he" or "I" demonstrates the use of an internal frame of reference. Rogers points out that some situations are genuinely difficult to perceive from the student's perspective, especially if the student is confused. At times all teachers will experience evaluative and diagnostic thoughts, but teachers beginning to use the nondirective interview are often concerned with themselves and concentrate on thinking about what they should do. They do not listen to the student. The strategy works only if the teacher enters the perceptual world of the student and leaves behind the more traditional external frame of reference. Developing an internal frame of reference is not easy to do at first, but it is essential if the teacher is to understand *with* the student, not merely *about* the student.

Nondirective counseling stresses the emotional elements of the situation more than the intellectual. That is, nondirective counseling strives for reorganization through the realm of feeling rather than emotional reorganization through intellectual approaches. Often, this view leads teachers who are considering adopting the nondirective stance to question the possibility of conflicting roles. How, they reason, can I be a disciplinarian, a referee, an instructor, and a friend—and also be a counselor implementing nondirective principles? One way of examining the problem of role conflict is to acknowledge that teachers' roles are changing as our conceptions of education evolve. The traditional notion of a teacher may indeed be primarily one of a disciplinarian, but this role is becoming less and less pervasive. It's probably fair to say that as the use of the learning environment becomes more "open" and "individualized," the role of counselor and the use of one-to-one conferences becomes more appropriate for the teacher.

Teacher Skills for the Nondirective Interview

The Nondirective Model demonstrates itself best through the teacher's manner of relating to the student. The teacher responds to the student through verbal and nonverbal communication. The teacher does not control but facilitates. The student is responsible for initiating and maintaining the contact. The teacher reflects and clarifies the student's concerns, rather than judging and evaluating the student. The teacher's role is carried out through four general techniques: (1) nondirective lead taking, (2) nondirective responses to feelings, (3) semidirective responses to feelings, and (4) directive counseling moves. Used judiciously by the teacher, these techniques facilitate the movement from release of feelings through insight to integration.

In the nondirective interview, the student bears the primary responsibility for the discussion; however, at times the teacher must make lead-taking responses in order to direct or maintain the conversation. Appropriate nondirective lead-taking responses are statements by the teacher that help get the interview going, or establish the direction in an open manner, or that give the student some indication as to what he or she should discuss, either specifically or generally. They may also be statements that explain what counseling is all about, or remarks that set the time and other limits of the interview. The essential skill in using this technique is to lead-take without assuming the basic responsibility for maintaining the interview. Nondirective lead-taking remarks are stated directly in a pleasant, positive, and amiable manner. Some examples are:

"What shall we talk about today?"

"What do you think of that?"

"Tell me more about it."

"How do you react when that happens?"

Nondirective responses to feelings are attempts to respond either to the feeling the student expresses or to the content of the expression. In making these comments, the teacher does not interpret, evaluate, or offer advice, but reflects, clarifies, accepts, and demonstrates understanding. The purpose of these comments is to create an atmosphere in which the student is willing to expand the ideas he is expressing. Usually, the responses are short statements that are supportive and enable the student to continue the discussion. Some examples are:

"Mm-hm." (nods)

"I see."

"It's especially hard to be alone."

"Sorta like it doesn't matter what you do, it will still go on the same way."

Semidirective responses to feelings can be thought of as directive, but they are used to a certain extent by nondirective counselors. There are two types of semidirective response: *interpretation* and *approval*. Both are used sparingly because they intrude on the nondirective style. But occasionally, they are useful in moving the interview forward.

An interpretation by the teacher can often promote further discussion by a student who is unable to offer any explanation for his behavior. Interpretative responses are attempts to suggest to the student his reasons when he is unable to continue the discussion. But interpretation is given only to those feelings that can definitely be accepted by the student. The decision to use interpretation is made cautiously by the teacher and is used only in situations where the teacher feels confident that interpretation will advance rather than close a dialogue. Some examples of interpretative openers are:

"You do this because. . ."

"Perhaps you feel you won't succeed."

"Your reasons for your actions this week are. . ."

"You are saying to me that the problem is. . ."

Approval statements evaluate the student or his idea; the teacher uses them to provide emotional support. Approval is usually given only when genuine progress has been achieved. It must occur sparingly, or the nondirective relationship is likely to drift rapidly into the traditional teacher-student relationship. Approval as a closure technique must be used with caution, or it may become a signal to the student that the interview is over. Other techniques, such as summarizing or recapping the session using the student's own words, are more appropriate to the nondirective strategy. In making approval statements, the teacher might say:

"That's right."

"That's a very interesting comment and may well be worth considering again."

"I really think you are in a good space now."

"That last idea was particularly strong. Could you elaborate on it some more?"

"I think we are really making progress together."

Directive counseling moves imply a relationship in which the teacher attempts to change the immediate ideas of the student or influence his attitudes. The teacher does this by giving support, expressing disapproval and criticism, giving information or explanations, proposing a solution, or attempting to convince the student. For example, "Don't you think it would be better if. . ." directly suggests a choice to the student. Attempts to support the student directly are usually made to reduce apparent anxiety, but they do not contribute to the nondirective problem-solving technique. Directive counseling moves should be used sparingly; otherwise, they can defeat the nondirective interview strategy. When utilizing directive counseling moves, the teacher maintains a more traditional role and does not help the student as an equal. The relationship remains traditional, and the teacher can easily become an authority figure and not a partner.

These four general techniques are supported by specific skills that enable the nondirective interviewer to act as a facilitator during the interview. These skills, which encourage the development of a direction to the interview or maintain the student's initiative in the interview, can be divided into two categories: (1) nondirective responses to feelings, by which the teacher reacts to the student's feelings, and (2) nondirective lead-taking responses, by which the teacher takes on leadership without removing the student's responsibility for initiative. These techniques develop from the nondirective view of the relationship between student and teacher.

Nondirective Responses in Interviews

The Nondirective Model assumes that behavior is not only rational, but that how we feel about ourselves, our goals, our capabilities, and our social context are important determinants of our behavior—and legitimately so. To solve most problems, we cannot simply "think them out"; we have to understand the role of our emotions and how they determine our goals and our patterns of behavior. The nondirective teacher must exercise a repertoire of responses that help the student understand the feelings and concerns he is experiencing and that encourage him to verbalize emotion he may feel unable to express. The teacher must do this in a way that accepts the student's frame of reference and student's responsibility for maintaining the conversation.

In order for the teacher to maintain the nondirective interview strategy, we will concentrate on eight responses that embody the nondirective stance. Three are nondirective responses to feelings and five are nondirective lead-taking moves. (See Figure 3.)

There is no particular pattern to the techniques used in the nondirective interview. Each is a skill for developing the internal frame of reference from which the teacher must operate in order to understand with the student as he formulates, explores, and resolves his problem or conflict. The focus and pace of the interviews are determined primarily by the student. But the maintenance of the nondirective responses and the avoidance of responses characteristic of more directive roles are essential to the implementation of a nondirective stance. Also, although there is not

I. Nondirective responses to feelings

    1. simple acceptance
    2. reflection of feelings
    3. paraphrasing of content

II. Nondirective lead-taking responses

    1. structuring
    2. directive questioning
    3. forcing student to choose and develop a topic
    4. nondirective leads and open questions
    5. minimal encouragements to talk

Figure 3. *Nondirective Responses in Interview.*

a rigid pattern to all counseling sessions, there is probably some kind of overall logic to the conversations. If it were not for some common elements, it would not be possible to have a "lore" or storehouse of counseling techniques. As it is, the common elements of counseling situations and the kinds of needs that these situations generate have made it possible for us to identify techniques that are useful in counseling.

Responses to Feelings

The three nondirective responses to feelings (simple acceptance, reflection of feeling, paraphrasing of context) represent the essence of the nondirective stance. They are the means by which the counselor conveys the attitudes of empathetic understanding and acceptance. Each of these techniques will be defined below, and examples will be given. As you read this material, think about how you could incorporate these techniques into your own teaching style.

Simple Acceptance. This consists of a brief statement indicating simple agreement, understanding, or assent, but not implying approval or disapproval in the judgmental sense. Simple acceptance conveys an "I am with you" attitude. Examples are: "I see," "I understand," "Hmm," "Uh-huh," a smile, a nod of the head, or even silence. These responses tend to encourage the student to continue talking or sharing ideas and feelings, but they do not "lead" the student. Once rapport has been established, simple acceptance comments can be very effective in generating further student comments. Below are two examples of the use of this technique.

Examples

S: I really want to go out for the tennis team, but I'm afraid I won't look good.
T: I see.

S: How do I deal with this? I really have trouble sleeping.
T: Uh-huh.

S: I can't seem to get any better, and I worry about it.
T: I understand.

S: I'm frightened about the math test.

T: Hmm.

S: Well, I'm really upset about this one. I'm really terrified about getting into college.

T: I see.

These examples point out the key idea of the teacher withholding judgment and allowing the student to explore and develop his own understanding of the problem. Simple acceptance is easily incorporated into most teaching styles. The idea is simply to give the student a chance to say more without evaluative comments from the teacher.

Reflection of Feelings. This response helps the student to become more aware of and to understand the feelings he is experiencing. Rarely do people describe their emotional states directly, by saying "I feel angry" or "I feel pleased." In fact, many people are unaware of their feelings or are embarrassed about discussing them.

Emotional states reveal themselves in many different ways—words, gestures, actions, tone of voice, and facial expressions. As nondirective counselor, the teacher must attend to all the cues that indicate the feelings of the student, focusing not only on what the student says (the content) but on *how* he says it. The student's feelings may be strong and explicit, confused and implicit, positive, negative, ambivalent, or directed towards other people, situations, or the student himself. When the student expresses ambivalent feelings, the teacher must reflect the ambivalent nature of the feelings without agreeing with one side or the other.

In using this technique, the teacher restates what the student may be feeling, hoping to clarify the student's view. However, merely changing the student's wording does not constitute clarification. Reflection reorganizes or synthesizes the feelings expressed by the student so that emotions can be better perceived and seen in their context. The following dialogue illustrates the use of reflection of feelings.

S: I feel really lousy.

T: What's the matter?

S: I'm the smallest one in the class, and every time we choose up sides for any kind of game I'm always picked last.

T: You feel lousy because being small, you're picked last?

S: Yeah, I feel lousy because of the connection between them.

T: You don't feel badly about being small or about being chosen last, but just about the connection?

S: Not exactly. I guess I feel badly about all three.

T: Are you trying to say that you want to be seen as a human being on your own terms and it's frustrating to be judged on the basis of your size?

S: Something like that.

T: It is as if you're simply a number, just the smallest number.

S: Yeah, I think so.

By reflecting this student's feelings, the teacher has begun to develop a rapport with the student so that he can begin to take on the real problem: dealing with his feelings at the same time that he tries to deal with the situation that has contributed to those feelings. In this example, the teacher helped clarify the student's underlying feelings by stating more concisely what was somewhat jumbled or unnamed in them, such as anger, resentment, and ambition. Reflection of feelings also serves to assure the student that his feelings are recognized and accepted, and serves to stimulate him to talk further on an issue. By selectively attending to the student's feelings, the teacher can help him explore a particular emotional state.

You should not try to respond reflectively to every comment by the student. Instead, use the simple acceptance techniques of smiling, nodding, or saying "Uh-huh" until there is an opportunity to reflect the feelings of the student. Premature reflection is based on very few cues and perhaps an inadequate understanding of the student's feelings. Also, it does not allow the student sufficient time to explore his ideas, and it often includes premature judgments.

EXERCISE 1

Organize yourselves into pairs. Each pair will practice generating simple acceptance and reflection of feeling responses while the others observe the process. The first member of the pair should attempt to state a problem, and the second member should attempt to provide a statement that either accepts or reflects the feelings about the problem in an honest but nonpunitive way. Check the sample dialogue above, and be sure that you are clear about the processes of simple acceptance and reflection of feelings. Each member of the pairs should identify a number of feelings that he or she might express. The members of each pair should take turns making statements and then trying to reflect these back to the other person. Finally, the members of the group should offer one another constructive comments focusing on the development of nondirective skills. As an aid in reviewing this material in the future, note here two of the problems that were offered, and the responses that were made to them.

Problem 1:   **Problem 2:**

Simple Acceptance: **Simple Acceptance:**

Reflection of Feeling: **Reflection of Feeling:**

Paraphrasing of Content. This is the third type of nondirective response to feeling. It is a means of clarifying the student's perceptions and letting him know that you are listening to him. In contrast with the reflection of feeling, the paraphrasing of content emphasizes more of the intellectual aspects of the student's communication than the feeling tone of it, the substantive content rather than the emotional content. By using a content *summary*, the teacher pulls together a number of the student's statements, a phase of the interview, or the entire interview. The paraphrasing of content integrates the cognitive elements of the student's discussion. It can also be used at the beginning of an interview by the teacher to open the session by recapping the key points of the previous session. The paraphrasing of content is appropriate when the student has expressed his ideas in a confused or rambling manner. In using this technique, the teacher condenses and succinctly expresses the student's thoughts. The teacher's facility in reflecting content allows for mutual assessment at the middle or end of the interview of what has been learned so far and what the next direction for the interview should be.

The variety of ways in which the teacher can paraphrase content is much more extensive than is the case with simple acceptance and reflection of feeling. However, the teacher needs to be aware of the manipulation that is possible with rephrasing. Faithfulness to the student's original meaning and intention is imperative in paraphrasing content.

Here is an example of how a teacher paraphrases (a nondirective lead-taking skill) and then shifts the responsibility back to the student.

S: I'd really like to play tennis better, but I just can't seem to work it out. I have trouble with lessons. My game seems to get worse for a long time before I get better. Lessons don't seem to help, but what else can I do?

T: You would like to improve your game, but lessons don't seem to do it. What other strategies come to mind?

The teacher listened to the problem and summarized it for the student, but he did not respond to the pupil's question, "What else can I do?" Instead, he shifted the direction for the interview back to the student.

EXERCISE 2

Along with the rest of your group, break into pairs, keeping or changing partners depending on group preferences. Each pair will generate a problem. Try to work through the problem using the three nondirective responses to feeling: simple acceptance, reflection of feeling, and paraphrasing of content. Try to combine all three skills. Limit your working through of the problem to seven to ten minutes. Note two of the problems and the responses that were offered below.

Problem 1:   Problem 2:

Simple Acceptance: Simple Acceptance:

Reflection of Feeling: Reflection of Feeling:

Paraphrasing of Content: Paraphrasing of Content:

Nondirective Lead-Taking

The three nondirective responses to feeling are skills that reflect the ideas, feelings, and problems of the student. In the role of counselor, however, the teacher is not inactive. The teacher has to help the student to bring up and deal with his ideas, feelings, and problems, while projecting an accepting and facilitative stance. The teacher's leadership function is delicate because the student has to be drawn out without the teacher becoming the leader of the process. But even though the responsibility for pacing and focusing the interview rests primarily with the student, the teacher has to develop techniques that prompt and aid the student in assuming this responsibility *without usurping it*. These techniques are called *nondirective lead-taking moves*. They have three functions: (1) to define the counseling context; (2) to prompt continuation or direction in the interview; and (3) to indicate to the student what should be discussed. We have identified five such moves:

1. structuring
2. direct questions
3. forcing student to choose and develop a topic
4. nondirective leads and open questions
5. minimal encouragement to talk

In the nondirective interview, these moves blend with the nondirective responses to feeling. Although we can isolate skills for practice in this text, a real nondirective interview moves rapidly and the different nondirective skills blend together in various combinations, depending on the needs of the situation. We hope that a careful reading of the various transcripts in the text will help you overcome some of the artificiality of using training material.

Structuring. This consists of statements that explain the counseling procedure, the time limitations, and the responsibilities of both the teacher and the student. Structuring comments are usually clear and to the point. Generally they occur only at the beginning of the interview. Here are two examples:

T: This is a time we can get together to talk about whatever you want. Whatever you choose to talk about is fine with me.

T: By talking together about this problem, we may be able to work out a solution that will satisfy both of us. Why don't you begin to tell me about the problem as you see it. I will listen.

Direct Questions. This is a technique in which the teacher asks for specific information. Sometimes the teacher uses a direct question to obtain specific examples of behavior in order that he or she can better understand what the student is saying. For example:

T: I'm not sure I heard you correctly. Did you say this is something your mother or your brother does?

T: Can you give me a specific example?

T: What do you mean when you say he is weird?

T: What do you do when you feel sad?

The teacher must use direct questions cautiously. They are intended to extend the interview, not to manipulate the student to accept a specific decision made by the teacher.

EXERCISE 3

Break the group into pairs, keeping or changing partners depending on group preferences. Identify a problem and use some structuring moves to begin the nondirective interview. Include nondirective responses to feelings, but in addition, blend in direct questions. Do not spend more than five to ten minutes on this exercise. Note two of the problems and the responses offered below.

Problem 1:   **Problem 2:**

Structuring: Structuring:

Simple Acceptance: Simple Acceptance:

Reflection of Feeling: Reflection of Feeling:

Paraphrasing of Content: Paraphrasing of Content:

Direct Questions: Direct Questions:

Forcing Student to Choose and Develop a Topic. This is a key skill. It shifts the responsibility for maintaining the interview to the student. Included here are all those responses by the teacher to student questions that attempt to reject responsibility for directing the interview. Students often ask questions when in fact they are requesting advice. When such questions are answered they usually produce additional questions; eventually, the reflective counseling session turns into a question-and-answer period that avoids real exploration of problems. Examples of questions that redirect to the student the responsibility for maintaining the content of the interview and solving his problems are:

T: Well, how do *you* feel about that?

T: What shall we talk about today?

T: You feel that's the problem?

      Nondirective Leads and Open Questions. Nondirective leads are teacher responses that invite comments and elicit *further* student statements of the problem. These responses avoid limiting the nature of the discussion to any narrow topic. They are designed to help the student clarify his problems further, not to furnish information for the teacher. Some examples are:

T: Tell me more about it.

T: What could you do differently?

T: How have things been since we last saw each other?

T: You mentioned that you feel your parents pressure you. Could you say more about that?

These leads encourage a direction without limiting the nature of the response except in a general way.

      Another way of describing these leads is as open questions, as opposed to closed questions. Open questions begin with How, What, Could, Can you tell me . . . . , Imagine that. . . . These stems are a good way to begin direct questions, forcing students to choose and develop a topic as well as open questions. However, the purposes of these three types of lead-taking are different.

      Open questions are used to begin an interview or to get the student to elaborate a point. In contrast, closed questions can often be answered in a few words or with a yes or a no, and are to be avoided. "Why" questions tend to make people defensive and should be avoided.

Open: Could you tell me a little more about your relationship with your brother?

Closed: Why can't you get along with your brother?
                  Do you want to get along better with your brother?

      Minimal Encouragements to Talk. This is the final leadership role that we will identify. Once the student has begun to talk, the teacher has to say very little in order to encourage him to continue. Often, one or two words will suffice. In this way, minimal encouragement is similar to the technique of simple acceptance. Minimal encouragement responses permit the student to maintain control of the interview but force him to elaborate, explain, or probe more deeply into the problem. In using this technique, the teacher accepts the student's comments and encourages greater focusing by the student on the problem. Examples of minimal encouragement responses are:

T: Oh?

T: So?

T: Then?

T: And?

Or the technique can consist of the repetition of one or two words. For instance, instead of asking the direct question, "What do you mean, your father is out of his mind?" the teacher could simply repeat, "Out of his mind?"

EXERCISE 4

Pick out a partner and choose a problem for a nondirective interview. Try to include all eight of the skills that have been outlined above. For your use in reviewing, make some notes in the space below.

Problem:

Simple Acceptance: Direct Questions:

Reflection of Feeling: Forcing Student to Choose and Develop a Topic:

Paraphrasing of Content: Nondirective Leads and Open Questions:

Structuring: Minimal Encouragement to Talk:

EXERCISE 5: PUTTING IT ALL TOGETHER

If you are able to complete Exercise 4 without any problems, you are ready for the final exercise. This exercise gives you an opportunity to test your diagnostic ability in the use of all eight nondirective responses. Several counseling situations are described below. For each one, determine the most appropriate type of teacher move (or moves) from the eight nondirective responses. Write down your choices, and check your answers in the key at the end of the exercise.

1. Student's comment at beginning of session indicates the achievement of genuine insight into his problem since the last meeting.

2. Student disagrees with teacher.

3. Student indicates negative attitude toward self.

4. Teacher wants to find out how student sees his situation.

5. Student is reticent about talking. Teacher wants to facilitate continuation of discussion during the interview.

6. Student describes a conflict between him and his brother. Teacher wants to avoid talking sides.

7. Student has exhausted a topic.

8. Teacher wants to convey empathy and understanding to student.

9. Review of previous session.

10. Mutual assessment in order to plan next steps.

11. Student states negative feelings toward others.

12. Student asks teacher's advice on his problem.

Key to Exercise 5: Putting It All Together

1. Probably paraphrasing of content. If the entire interview was filled with insight, perhaps some open statement of approval, such as, "I can see you've been doing a lot of thinking."
2. Paraphrasing of content.
3. Reflection of feeling.
4. Open question.
5. Reflection of feeling or minimal encouragement.
6. Reflection of feeling.
7. Reflection of feeling or summary; paraphrasing.
8. Reflection of feeling and simple acceptance.
9. Summary reflection of feeling and content.
10. Summary reflection of feeling and content.
11. Simple acceptance or reflection of feeling.
12. Reflection of feeling.

THEORY CHECKUP FOR THE NONDIRECTIVE MODEL

1. Which of the following statements agree with the role of the teacher in the Nondirective Model of teaching?
   a. Teacher should be the only decision-maker in the class.
   b. Teacher should accept student self-assessment of problems.
   c. Teacher should function to help students develop cognitively.
   d. Teacher should not be concerned with perceiving the classroom as the student sees it.
   e. Teacher should not assert own bias in a nondirective interview.

2. Which technique would a teacher or facilitator use to begin a nondirective interview?

3. Which technique would a teacher use to "say back" to a student what he or she has said?

4. List the five phases of a Nondirective Teaching strategy.
   a.
   b.
   c.
   d.
   e.

5. Give two examples of simple acceptance statements.
   a.
   b.

6. What are the four phases of the personal growth process?
   a.
   b.
   c.
   d.

7. What physical arrangement is most conducive to effective use of the Nondirective Teaching strategy?

8. When are direct questions appropriate?

9. Which of the following situations would be appropriate for classroom use of nondirective interview techniques?
   a. performance contracts
   b. problems of tardiness
   c. severe social or emotional problems
   d. conflict with another student in class
   e. group assignments in class
   f. evaluation of student work

10. What is the difference between open and closed questions?

Key to Theory Checkup

1. a. no
   b. yes
   c. no
   d. no
   e. yes

2. Structuring

3. Paraphrase
4. a. Helping situation is defined
   b. Encouraging students
   c. Developing insight
   d. Planning and decision-making
   e. Integration
5. a. "I see."
   b. "I understand."
6. a. Release of feeling or catharsis
   b. Insight
   c. Action
   d. Integration
7. A quiet, private place where the student will feel comfortable to express his or her ideas and feelings.
8. Direct questions are appropriate to extend the interview, to obtain specific examples, and to help focus the interview in order to better understand the student.
9. a. yes
   b. yes
   c. no
   d. yes
   e. yes
   f. yes
10. Closed questions can be answered in a single word or several words. Open questions require that student expand and develop previous statements.

Component II

VIEWING
THE MODEL

One of the purposes of Component II is to provide examples of actual sessions in which the Nondirective Model is the strategy being used. Reading the demonstration transcript that follows, hearing a tape of a teacher and students, or viewing a filmstrip of class activity are alternative means of illustrating the "model in action."

As you study any of these alternatives, you will be introduced to the Teaching Analysis Guide for analyzing the model. This same Guide will also be used in Component III to analyze the peer teaching and microteaching lessons. We want you to become familiar with the Guide now, however, as it will sharpen your perception of the demonstration lesson.

The two activities in this component are (1) reading the Teaching Analysis Guide and (2) viewing (reading) the lesson. Before going on to them, you may wish to reread the material in the Introduction to this book that discusses the purposes and philosophy of the Teaching Analysis Guide.

TEACHING ANALYSIS GUIDE FOR NONDIRECTIVE TEACHING

This Guide is to be used as you observe demonstrations of Nondirective Teaching and analyze your peer teaching and that of others. It will also be used for microteaching (teaching small groups of children) and for general classroom observation.

The Guide emphasizes what we consider to be the essential features of the Nondirective stance. With some models of teaching, the Guide can specify particular teaching skills and definitive phases of the model. In Nondirective Teaching, however, the learner participates so fully in the determination of events that no prescribed sequence can be made, and the counseling interview can turn out in a variety of ways. Thus, this guide is designed to help you look for particular dimensions of Nondirective Teaching and to determine if the person being observed— whether yourself or someone else—is dealing with those dimensions.

The Problematic Dimension

In most school situations, Nondirective Teaching occurs because there is a problem that is perceived by the student or the teacher. Unless the problem—or at least the student's feelings about the problem—is explored, Nondirective Teaching can wander in circles. In the space below, indicate your observations about the teacher's ability to help the student define the problem in cognitive and affective terms and reflect to himself where he stands in the problem area. Then, in the rating form to the right, judge the adequacy with which the teacher fulfilled this dimension of Nondirective Teaching.

Thoroughly	Partially	Missing	Not Needed

Maintaining an Equal Role

One of the essential features of Nondirective Teaching is maintaining an egalitarian relationship with the student. In the interview, the teacher is definitely the teacher, just as a counselor is definitely a counselor, but this role implies *function* rather than *status*. If the teacher gives greater weight to his or her own ideas than to the student's ideas, the relationship that is essential for nondirection is destroyed. The teacher may provide ideas or wisdom, but is not to be superior. In the space below, jot down your general assessment of the teacher's ability to maintain an egalitarian stance. Then provide a rating.

Thoroughly	Partially	Missing	Not Needed

139

TEACHING ANALYSIS GUIDE FOR NONDIRECTIVE TEACHING

The Nondirective Dimension

Did the teacher maintain a relatively nondirective stance? That is, did the teacher seek the frame of reference of the student and help the student to understand himself in relation to the problem under consideration? This stance contrasts sharply with an instructive stance, where the teacher seeks an opportunity to provide information or ideas external to the student's frame of reference. Nondirection means exactly that. The teacher is not there to direct, but to facilitate. The teacher may take the lead at times, but primarily to help the student understand himself and come to grips with his own problems rather than to provide information or concepts that are unrelated to the student's self-concept and perception of his world. Comment below on the success of the teacher in upholding the nondirective dimension, and then supply a rating.

Thoroughly   Partially   Missing   Not
Needed

Expression of Feelings

The expression of feelings (often referred to as catharsis) enables the learner to vent his emotions and begin to come to grips with himself as an emotional as well as a cognitive being. Without the expression of feelings, Nondirective Teaching is dry and empty. In the space below, put down your observations about the ability of the teacher to elicit feelings from the learner, to accept them, and to encourage their expression while helping the student understand them. Then provide a rating.

Thoroughly   Partially   Missing   Not
Needed

The Skills Dimensions

Reflecting, probing, and lead taking are among the specific skills that aid the facilitative process of Nondirective Teaching. Various skills are needed at various times. Indicate in the space below the kinds of skills that the teacher used and your view of the extent to which the teacher was able to use them appropriately and strongly. In the rating form to the right, indicate the adequacy with which you feel the teacher displayed the skills called for by the nondirective stance.

Thoroughly   Partially   Missing   Not
Needed

140

TEACHING ANALYSIS GUIDE FOR NONDIRECTIVE TEACHING

Next Steps

Nondirective interviews often seem somewhat inconclusive in contrast with instructional encounters. Nonetheless, the student comes to the nondirective interview to learn, as much as he comes to directive instruction to learn. One of the most important dimensions in a successful interview is the establishment of a common frame of reference between teacher and learner that leads to future interviews or helps the individual develop a way of approaching his future. What we are concerned with here is the establishment, at some point, of a reasonable focus for the learner. He should become aware of his feelings, or of a better definition of the problem, or of something he is going to work on before the next interview. In the space below, comment on how successfully a common frame of reference was established that would lead to follow-up steps. Judge the adequacy with which a theme was established that could provide continuity as the learner struggles with his problems.

Thoroughly	Partially	Missing	Not Needed

DEMONSTRATION TRANSCRIPT: NONDIRECTIVE MODEL

In this transcript of an actual classroom dialogue, a leader poses a problem for discussion by the class. The complexity of modern schooling and its impact on students is the topic of the discussion. The students work out their ideas by responding to one another. After the initial structuring the leader withdraws, intruding thereafter only for support or clarification.

T: MY ROLE IS TO SET A THEME, AND THEN YOU INTERACT WITH RESPECT TO THAT. THE ISSUE IS THAT IN A COMPLICATED TECHNOLOGICAL SOCIETY LIKE THIS ONE, MOST OF US BEAR A LIFELONG RELATIONSHIP WITH EDUCATION OR CHANGE CAREERS MANY TIMES. I HAVEN'T BEEN ABLE TO GET AWAY FROM GOING TO SCHOOL FOR SOME TIME.

Phase One: Helping Situation Is Defined
Structuring: nondirective stance and introduction of problem for discussion

S: MIGHT AS WELL.

T: IN FACT, I THINK IT'S FORTY YEARS SINCE I STARTED GOING TO SCHOOL. I THINK SOME DAYS THAT I'M DOING MORE NOW THAN I EVER DID, AND MORE INTENSIVELY. AND IT'S PRETTY WELL TRUE ABOUT MANY, MANY PEOPLE. WHAT WE'RE LIVING IN RIGHT NOW IS IN THIS BIG FLOW OF AN EDUCATIONAL SYSTEM THAT'S ALL AROUND US. WE RELATE TO IT IN DIFFERENT WAYS. PART OF THAT RELATIONSHIP IS NOT OF OUR CHOOSING. ONE KIND OF NONCHOICE IS WHERE WE ARE MANDATED IN THE SCHOOL—WHERE YOU MUST GO UNTIL YOU ARE SIXTEEN OR EIGHTEEN OR WHATEVER. AND THE SECOND IS, THINGS LIKE ECONOMIC NECESSITY DRIVE US TOWARD IT, SO IT BECOMES ALMOST MANDATORY FOR US, EVEN

Maintaining an equal role: leader establishes problem within students' context

THOUGH IT ISN'T LEGISLATED, TO ACHIEVE REASONABLE LEVELS OF IT. SO THAT'S THE SETTING. THE THEME OR THE PROBLEM THAT EACH OF US FACES IS, HOW DO WE FEEL ABOUT THE SYSTEM THAT WE ARE PART OF? HOW DO WE INTEND TO USE IT? WHAT ARE THE PURPOSES OF THE SYSTEM THAT WE'RE PART OF? WHAT ARE OUR PERSONAL ISSUES IN RELATION TO IT? THEY'RE PRETTY MUCH THE SAME. THAT'S WHY WE CAN DISCUSS IT IN A GROUP, EVEN THOUGH EACH INDIVIDUAL SOLVES HIS OWN SPECIFIC PROBLEMS IN HIS OWN WAY. SO, THE QUESTION I PUT ON THE TABLE FOR YOU IS, "HOW SHOULD WE RELATE TO THE EDUCATIONAL SYSTEM?" WHAT IS ITS CHARACTER, YOU KNOW? WHAT ARE ITS PROBLEMS? WHAT ARE THE PROBLEMS IN RELATING TO IT?   *Open question*

S: WELL, WE REALLY DON'T HAVE ANY CHOICE UNTIL WE'RE SIXTEEN OR EIGHTEEN.

T: WHAT ARE YOU GOING TO DO NOW? YOU'RE REACHING THE END OF THE MANDATED PART. HOW ARE YOU GOING TO LOOK AT THIS FROM NOW ON?   **Phase Two: Exploration of Problem**

S: HOW DO I GET AWAY? I DON'T KNOW ANYTHING ELSE EXCEPT GOING TO SCHOOL AFTER YOU GET OUT OF THERE.

T: WE GET SOCIAL PARTICIPATION BY ACHIEVEMENT IN EDUCATION.   *Paraphrase*

S: THERE IS NO OTHER CLEARLY DEFINED CHOICE OR DESIRABLE ALTERNATIVE OTHER THAN GOING TO SCHOOL.

S: YOU CAN WORK.

S: THERE'S NOTHING I WANT TO DO RIGHT NOW.

S: THE MOST GENERAL PROBLEM IS THAT IT'S A SOMEWHAT IMPERSONAL SYSTEM.

S: WELL, I SUPPOSE THE REST OF US PROBABLY FEEL, WE'RE REALLY BREAKING OUR BACKS TO GET GOOD GRADES IN SCHOOL—

T: UH-HUH.   *Minimal acceptance*

S: —AND AFTERWARD WE'RE READY TO CRY.

T: UH-HUH.

S: SO YOU CAN BREAK YOUR BACK AND GET A GOOD JOB AND, YOU KNOW, BY THE TIME YOU'RE SIXTY-FIVE, ALL YOU HAVE IS A BROKEN BACK.   *Paraphrase*

S: YEAH.

S: I DON'T KNOW, I JUST CAN'T SEE GOING TO THAT EFFORT.

S: I THINK IT'S FOR A PLACE TO BE.

S: WELL, ONCE YOU GET OUT, WHAT DO YOU DO?   *Expression of feeling*

S: THAT'S RIGHT. I JUST READ AN ARTICLE THE OTHER DAY THAT'S GUARANTEED TO SCARE YOU. I'M NOT GOING TO FACE IT; IT'S NOT ALWAYS THIS BAD. (laughter)

T: SOME DAYS WE'RE PRETTY SURE WE'LL BE THE ONE TO GET THE JOB, AND OTHER DAYS IT'S HOPELESS.

Reflection of feeling

T: BUT IT'S PART OF THE RECURRENT DILEMMA, BECAUSE OF OUR ECONOMIC AMBITIONS. WOULD COLLEGE BE DIFFERENT? IS IT REALLY NOW AN IMPERSONAL SYSTEM?

Phase Three: Developing Insight

Directive question

S: I CAN SEE EXTREMES WHERE IT WOULD BE A LOT MORE PERSONAL.

S: YOU KNOW, I THINK IT'S ALL—OUR EDUCATION. HIGH SCHOOL IS ABOUT AS PERSONAL AS YOU CAN GET.

T: HOW ABOUT KNOWLEDGE-WISE? DO YOU FIND THAT YOU ARE WISHING THE FUTURE WERE CLEARER? OR DO YOU FIND THAT YOU WISH THAT CHOICES DIDN'T HAVE TO BE MADE? GET INTO A GENERAL CURRICULUM FOR THREE OR FOUR YEARS AND CONTINUE TO EDUCATE YOUR-SELF, AND THEN MAKE CHOICES?

S: NO, NOT REALLY.

T: DO YOU FEEL A SENSE OF IMPENDING CHOICE? HOW DO YOU FEEL?

S: I JUST FEEL, REGARDLESS OF THE CHOICES YOU MAKE WHILE YOU'RE IN A FOUR-YEAR INSTITU-TION, WHEN YOU'RE THROUGH WITH IT, THEN IT JUST AMOUNTS TO NOTHING. UNLESS YOU CAN BE IN THE TOP THREE OF HARVARD'S CLASS, YOU'RE NOT GOING TO GET A JOB. YOU KNOW, I'VE GOT THIS FEELING THAT THERE'S A REAL SQUEEZE AND IT'S GETTING WORSE.

S: YEAH, BUT EVEN WORSE. I MEAN THERE'S NO ONE WHO'S GOING TO GET JOBS UNLESS—

T: SO THE TREADMILL GETS LONGER AND LONGER, AND YOU IMAGINE COLLEGE NOT COUNTING FOR ANYTHING ECONOMICALLY. IN ORDER TO HAVE A NICHE IN THE WORLD THERE'S GRADUATE SCHOOL AND THEN POST-GRADUATE AND THEN FINALLY, IF YOU CAN SQUEEZE OUT THE OTHER END, YOU GET ONE OF THE SIX POSITIONS.

Paraphrasing of content
Summarizing

S: I DON'T THINK IT'S ALL MONEY-ORIENTED.

S: I DON'T THINK ANYONE HERE IS REALLY, YOU KNOW, GOING TO COLLEGE IN ORDER TO GET, YOU KNOW, THE ENGINEERING DEGREE IN OR-DER TO MAKE A MILLION IN FIVE YEARS.

T: UH-HUH.

Simple acceptance: encourages student re-sponses

S: BUT I'M INTERESTED IN, FOR INSTANCE, GETTING AN ENGINEERING DEGREE SO THAT I CAN GET A JOB AS AN ENGINEER SO I CAN BE DOING SOME-THING THAT I MIGHT WANT TO BE DOING FOR THE REST OF MY LIFE.

T: UH-HUH.

S: IN OTHER WORDS, BECAUSE I WANT TO BE AN ENGINEER.

S: FOR SOME SATISFACTION.

S: NOT BECAUSE I WANT TO BE RICH.

S: I'M MORE INTERESTED IN GETTING EDUCATED AND, IN THE PROCESS, PICKING UP SOME SORT OF SKILLS WHICH WILL ALLOW ME TO SURVIVE.

S: I WANT TO FIND THAT SOMEBODY SURVIVED AND IF I'M GOING TO FIND THAT, I GUESS I'LL HAVE TO BE EDUCATED TO FIND OUT. THERE'S NO WAY YOU CAN MISS ON EDUCATION.

T: UH-HUH.

S: YEAH, WELL, MY NATURE, I WON'T MISS BEING EDUCATED.

T: UH-HUH. IN TERMS OF THE SYSTEM YOU'RE JUST FINISHING, HOW WOULD YOU CHANGE IT TO MAKE IT BETTER IN TERMS OF YOURSELVES?

Open question

S: I WAS THINKING ABOUT THAT EVER SINCE SEVENTH GRADE. (laughter)

S: I DIDN'T COME TO ANY CONCLUSIONS. IT'S HARD TO EDUCATE EVERYONE. IT'S IMPOSSIBLE WHEN YOU DO IT ON A MASS BASIS. THERE ARE AN AWFUL LOT OF THINGS THAT COULD BE CHANGED. A LOT MORE FREEDOM, ELIMINATE GRADES ENTIRELY, NOT SO MUCH REPETITIOUS WORK, MORE CREATIVE WORK, NOT RESTRICTED TO THE CLASSROOM—I GUESS THAT'S ALL.

S: PART OF THE PROBLEM WITH MASS EDUCATION RIGHT NOW IS OVEREDUCATION. THERE ARE TWO WAYS TO RESPOND TO THAT. THERE ARE TOO MANY PEOPLE WHO ARE GOING ON TO HIGHER EDUCATION, MORE THAN WE NEED, AND ALSO WE'RE OVEREDUCATING, IN THAT WE'RE EDUCATING IN SORT OF THE WRONG THINGS. I MEAN, I'M NOT GOING TO REMEMBER—I TOOK CHEMISTRY LAST YEAR AND I COULDN'T TELL YOU ANYTHING.

T: UH-HUH.

S: I MEAN, YOU KNOW, OF ANY GREAT, IMPORTANT THESES—SOMEBODY CAN SAY SOMETHING, AND I'LL SAY, "OH, YEAH, YEAH, I DID SOMETHING LIKE THAT LAST YEAR."

T: UH-HUH.

S: AND, THERE WAS REALLY NO POINT IN IT. I MEAN, NOW I'M WELL ROUNDED.

T: UH-HUH.

S: BUT A LOT OF GOOD IT DOES ME.

T: UH-HUH. SO, IN A SENSE IT'S NOT RICH ENOUGH OR VIGOROUS ENOUGH ON A CERTAIN LEVEL. WE'RE OVEREDUCATED ON ONE LEVEL, AND IN OTHERS, IT'S EMPTY.

Reflection of feeling and paraphrasing content

S: IT'S TOO TECHNICAL, AT SOME LEVELS. IT'S NOT EDUCATION FOR A LIVING.

T: UH-HUH.

S: OR FOR USING.

T: UH-HUH.

S: IT'S FOR FORGETTING.

S: WHAT SHE JUST SAID, YOU CAN GO THE OTHER WAY. FOR SOMEBODY WHO IS TECHNICALLY ORIENTED. AND TAKES AN ENGLISH CLASS, AND SAYS, "WHY DO I HAVE TO LEARN ENGLISH?"

T: UH-HUH.

S: IT'S NO USE. SO I THINK EDUCATION SHOULD BE WELL ROUNDED FOR EVERYONE. MAYBE NOT BE REQUIRED—

S: —BUT SORT OF FORCED.

T: OK, IF YOU COME BACK TO THE KIND OF STANCE WE WERE IN BEFORE, WHAT SHOULD I BE DOING, AS A COLLEGE FACULTY MEMBER, TO MAKE THIS MAKE MORE SENSE?

S: COLLEGE?

T: YEAH, I'M A COLLEGE FACULTY MEMBER.

S: SO YOU CAN TEACH OTHERS.

S: WE'RE HELPING HIM CHANGE THE SYSTEM.

S: AHA.

T: OR MODIFY MY OWN BEHAVIOR.

S: WHICH IS PART OF THE SYSTEM.

T: HMM—YES.

S: HERE IN THE UNITED STATES.

S: I'D DISCOURAGE COMPETITION. AIM AT LEARNING RATHER THAN, WELL, GRADES.

T: SHOULD I BE WILLING TO TEACH CLASSES OF SAY, TWO HUNDRED?

S: SURE. EVEN THOSE KINDS OF CLASSES, THEY HAVE THEIR—THEY HAVE THEIR OWN KIND OF BENEFITS. YOU KNOW, YOU DON'T ALWAYS HAVE TO KNOW YOUR OWN TEACHER.

T: UH-HUH.

S: I THINK YOU SHOULD BE WILLING TO DEVOTE AT LEAST AS MUCH TIME AND EFFORT TO YOUR UNDERGRADUATE STUDENTS AS TO YOUR GRADUATE STUDENTS.

S: THAT'S BECAUSE YOU'RE GOING TO BE AN UNDERGRADUATE.

S: UH-HUH, RIGHT.

S: WELL, AN EDUCATION SHOULD BE MORE. I'VE DONE SOME OF MY OWN READING ON THE SIDE—

T: UH-HUH.

S: —BUT, ANYWAY, THERE'S QUITE A FOLLOWING FOR GLOBAL EDUCATION—

T: UH-HUH.

S: —AN APPRECIATION FOR BEING AN INTER-RELATED COMMUNITY—

T: UH-HUH.

S: —AND YOU NEED TO WORK AS A COMMUNITY MEMBER—

Phase Four: Planning and Decision Making

Simple acceptance

T: UH-HUH.

S: —AND, AND TO GET ALONG.

T: SHOULD WE—DO YOU THINK THAT THEY OUGHT TO REQUIRE, AS PART OF THE COLLEGE CURRICULUM, SAY, THE STUDY OF OTHER PEOPLE IN OTHER CULTURES? IS THAT REALISTIC?

Phase Five: Integration

Open questions

S: NO. IF I WANT TO BE AN ENGINEER, I—IF I REALLY WANT TO BE AN ENGINEER, I DON'T WANT SOME PROFESSOR TELLING ME I HAVE TO STUDY GREEK ZOOLOGY.

T: WELL, HOW ABOUT MODERN THEN.

Forcing student to develop topic

S: AT THE HIGH SCHOOL LEVEL I CAN SEE IT. BUT, YOU KNOW, I THINK THAT PEOPLE HAVE THE RIGHT TO MAKE THEIR OWN CHOICES ACADEMICALLY.

T: WELL, SHOULD THE COLLEGE SIMPLY REFLECT THE ACADEMIC AND ECONOMIC SYSTEM? I MEAN, THIS BUSINESS OF EVERYBODY GETTING IN PREMED. OR SHOULD THE COLLEGE TAKE A MORE OR LESS RADICAL STAND TOWARD THE SOCIETY? SHOULD IT BE REVISIONARY OR TRY TO TRAIN PEOPLE TO BE REVISIONARY?

Open question

S: I ALWAYS THOUGHT THAT THE PURPOSE OF EDUCATION IN GENERAL WAS JUST TO TEACH YOU HOW—NOT WHAT TO THINK BUT HOW TO THINK—

T: UH-HUH.

S: COLLEGE SHOULD BE SIMPLY AN EXTENSION OF TEACHING YOU HOW TO USE FACTS THAT ARE THERE.

T: UH-HUH.

S: WELL, AT SOME POINT YOU HAVE TO, IF YOU WANT TO BE AN ENGINEER—

S: YEAH, BUT THAT'S NOT THE END.

S: —TO BECOME SPECIALIZED, AND BY THE TIME YOU GET THROUGH GRADUATE SCHOOL YOU SHOULD KNOW SOMETHING SPECIFIC.

S: YEAH, BUT THAT'S NOT THE END IN ITSELF

T: OK. WHAT WE WERE TALKING ABOUT EARLIER— ROBERT HUTCHINS USED TO SAY, AND HE WAS THE PRESIDENT OF THE UNIVERSITY OF CHICAGO FOR MANY YEARS, AND WAS THE HEAD OF THE CENTER FOR THE STUDY OF DEMOCRATIC INSTITUTIONS—AND HIS STANCE USED TO BE THAT, KIND OF A ONE FROM PLATO. NOW PLATO WAS TRYING TO BUILD A SYSTEM TO EDUCATE THE GOVERNMENT, AND THE PINNACLE OF THE SYSTEM, THE GOVERNOR, HAD ALL KINDS OF EDUCATION. HUTCHINS SAID THAT EVERYBODY IN OUR SOCIETY, EVERYBODY IS A GOVERNOR IN ONE SENSE OR ANOTHER. AND, THEREFORE, THEY OUGHT TO ALSO ALL HAVE THE EDUCATION OF GOVERNORS. AT LEAST CERTAINLY THOSE WHO GO TO COLLEGE. AND, THEREFORE, THINGS LIKE UNDERSTANDING POWER, COM-

Structuring

PREHENDING THE GLOBAL ECOSYSTEM, KNOW-
ING THE MAINSTREAMS OF PHILOSOPHICAL AND
LITERARY THOUGHT, UNDERSTANDING POLIT-
ICAL SYSTEMS AND HOW TO CHANGE THEM,
AND THAT KIND OF STUFF BECAME REQUIRED
OF EVERYBODY. HE SAID THAT THE FUNCTION
OF DOING THIS IS TO ENABLE EVERYBODY TO
ENGAGE IN THE GREAT DIALOGUE THAT SOC-
RATES BEGAN, WHICH IS WHAT SHOULD BE THE
NATURE OF THE GOOD LIFE? AND WITH THAT
STANCE WE WOULD REQUIRE THINGS. IN THIS
CASE, THEY REQUIRED ONE HUNDRED BOOKS.

S: YEAH, THE GREAT BOOKS.

T: THE GREAT BOOKS. THAT'S INTERESTING.
SHOULD WE LET ANYBODY GET THROUGH WITH-
OUT THEM?

S: WELL, THOSE THINGS AREN'T REQUIRED OF YOU
ONCE YOU'RE OUT OF COLLEGE. YOU AREN'T
REQUIRED TO HAVE A DEEP UNDERSTANDING OF
THE GLOBAL ECOSYSTEMS, YOU KNOW. WHY
LEARN IT IN COLLEGE?

T: BECAUSE THE FACULTY, IN ALL ITS RIGHTEOUS-
NESS, MIGHT BELIEVE THAT IT WOULD BE GOOD
FOR YOU.

S: YUCK!

T: THE WORLD WOULD BE BETTER OFF IF EVERY-
BODY DID UNDERSTAND THOSE THINGS, EITHER
PURELY OR INCLUDING PHILOSOPHICAL AND
SOCIAL ISSUES.

S: I THINK IT'S REALLY TRUE THAT TO GET AN
EDUCATION, ONE NEEDS TO UNDERSTAND THOSE
THINGS, AND PRESENTLY WE HAVE A LOT OF
SCIENTISTS WHO ARE VERY, VERY GOOD SCIEN-
TISTS BUT HAVEN'T HAD THIS EDUCATION.

Component III

PLANNING
AND
PEER TEACHING

The focus of this component is on helping you practice the nondirective interview strategy. A partner is necessary. Pair off with someone else in your group. Having a partner will allow the two of you to practice with each other, comment on each other's progress, and monitor each other's success with the model. But if it is not possible to work with another adult, you may begin with a student.

It will be helpful to record your peer teaching lesson on audio tape. The nondirective responses are unfamiliar to most teachers, and the use of tape will facilitate your analysis of the lesson and help you to improve your skills. Listening to your responses will facilitate a sharper analysis of the nondirective strategy than trying to remember how you did at different stages during the interview. In addition, the tape will allow you to concentrate all of your attention on listening to your partner and reduce your attention to yourself and your responses.

The topics suitable for a nondirective interview are many and varied. Any personal or social interaction problem can be explored. Often, people choose to discuss problems with family or friends, or personal concerns. If you are working with another teacher, you may want to focus your interview on difficult relationships you may be having with students, teachers, or administrators in your school. If you work with a student, he or she will focus the problem. If you are unable to work with a partner, you will have to project possible problems and responses in the first section of this component.

The steps in planning the Nondirective Model are:

1. selecting and describing a problem
2. determining educational objectives
3. completing the Planning Guide
4. peer teaching
5. analyzing the peer teaching lesson
6. after peer teaching: microteaching

SELECTING AND DESCRIBING A PROBLEM

Using the nondirective interview strategy requires sensitivity on the part of the person functioning as counselor. Although it is not possible to identify problems before the interview begins, the sensitive counselor should be able to predict types of problems that are common among students.

EXERCISE 1

If you are working with peers, pause here and list some typical problems that students might bring up in an interview. You may be specific or general. If you are working alone, list as many problems as you can; the process will be the same, but you will not receive any feedback from your colleagues on your ideas.

How common do you think these problems are with adults? List some common problems that adults might bring to a counseling interview.

Can you see strands of emotional difficulties connecting your lists of student and adult problems? People often seek counseling help when they cannot cope with pressures or stresses resulting from their relationships with family or friends, or when they are feeling strained in their relationships with colleagues at work. For students, school is their work, and boredom, lack of interest, and frustration are problems that are common to students as well as to adults. If you are working with a partner, select the problems each of you would like to discuss and record them in the Planning Guide. If you are working with a student, discuss the strategy with the student before you begin the nondirective interview. From your initial discussion, you should be able to discern topics that are important to the student. Your interview will not necessarily be confined to these topics, but they will give you a start. List the topics in the Planning Guide.

DETERMINING EDUCATIONAL OBJECTIVES

The objectives of the Nondirective Model are affective in nature. Although changes in students' attitudes and in their outlook on life may be reflected in their schoolwork, the Nondirective Model concentrates on personal rather than intellectual objectives. If learning to be prompt helps a student complete more assignments on time, this is commendable. But a broader goal is to help the student understand his motivations so that he can cope with his problems, not just as a student, but as a member of a family and a community.

Often, the objectives of the nondirective strategy are stated in a negative form: help the student to stop doing something, and he will be better. Objectives that focus on positive behavioral change are more effective and show a more accepting approach by the teacher. Positive objectives also tend to be broader and concentrate on eliciting a new behavior pattern, not merely eliminating an old pattern.

EXERCISE 2

Using your list of common adult problems, develop a list of three objectives appropriate for affective change through the nondirective interview strategy.

If you are working with a partner, write two affective educational objectives for your counseling topic and two for your partner's topic. Have your partner do the same for you. List these objectives in the Planning Guide. If you are working with a student, consider your precounseling interview. From this discussion, list two or three affective objectives in the Planning Guide. Remember to concentrate on objectives that are concerned with eliciting positive changes.

Completing the Planning Guide

We have developed a Planning Guide in order to help you organize your nondirective interview. The Guide is especially helpful the first few occasions you use the Nondirective Model. After that, you may not have to plan so extensively.

Unlike other models, which concentrate on identified cognitive information in the Planning Guide, the Nondirective Model emphasizes emergent content, which is shorter and leaves more to your judgment. For this reason, the use of the Teaching Analysis Guide is particularly important with this model. It will help you judge how effectively you have used the nondirective interview responses—that is, the nondirective responses to feelings and the nondirective lead-taking responses.

By now, you should have completed Parts I and II of the Planning Guide. The remaining part asks you to (1) identify your opening moves for each phase and (2) identify appropriate nondirective responses that could be used with each phase. Complete Part III of the Guide now.

PLANNING GUIDE FOR THE NONDIRECTIVE MODEL

I. Selecting and Describing a Problem
    A. Peer teaching with a colleague
        1. My counseling topic:

        2. My partner's counseling topic:

    B. Microteaching with a student
        1. First counseling topic for student:

        2. Alternative counseling topic for student:

II. Determining Educational Objectives
    A. Peer teaching with a colleague
        1. My educational objective(s):
            a.
            b.
        2. My partner's educational objective(s):
            a.
            b.
    B. Microteaching with a student: educational objectives:
        1.
        2.
        3.

III. Determining Opening Moves for Each Phase and Identifying Appropriate Nondirective Responses
    Write your opening moves for each phase of the model and then check the more appropriate responses.

Opening moves for Phase One (Helping Situation Is Defined):

	Responses to Feelings		Nondirective Lead-Taking Responses
	simple acceptance		structuring
	reflection of feelings		directive questioning
			forcing student to choose and develop a topic
	paraphrasing of content		nondirective leads and open questions
			minimal encouragement to talk

Opening moves for Phase Two (Stating and Exploring the Problem; Expression and Clarification of Feelings):

	Responses to Feelings		Nondirective Lead-Taking Responses
	simple acceptance		structuring
	reflection of feelings		directive questioning
			forcing student to choose and develop a topic
	paraphrasing of content		nondirective leads and open questions
			minimal encouragement to talk

Opening moves for Phase Three (Discussion of Student Feelings: Developing Insight):

	Responses to Feelings		Nondirective Lead-Taking Responses
	simple acceptance		structuring
	reflection of feelings		directive questioning
			forcing student to choose and develop a topic
	paraphrasing of content		nondirective leads and open questions
			minimal encouragement to talk

Opening moves for Phase Four (Student Planning and Decision Making):

	Responses to Feelings		Nondirective Lead-Taking Responses
	simple acceptance		structuring
	reflection of feelings		directive questioning
			forcing student to choose and develop a topic
	paraphrasing of content		nondirective leads and open questions
			minimal encouragement to talk

Opening moves for Phase Five (Integration; Positive Insight and Action):

	Responses to Feelings		Nondirective Lead-Taking Responses
	simple acceptance		structuring
	reflection of feelings		directive questioning
			forcing student to choose and develop a topic
	paraphrasing of content		nondirective leads and open questions
			minimal encouragement to talk

ANALYZING THE PEER TEACHING LESSON

As soon as you have completed your nondirective interview with a partner or a student, complete the Teaching Analysis Guide that follows. Duplicate as many copies of the Guide as may be needed to analyze the peer teaching and microteaching of all members of the group. It would be best if you could listen to an audio tape of your interview as well. The *sound* of your responses is as important as the responses themselves. You want to convey, not just through your words but through your tone, that you are a receptive listener.

Record below the nondirective responses you may need to use or improve upon next time.

TEACHING ANALYSIS GUIDE FOR NONDIRECTIVE TEACHING

This Guide is to be used as you observe demonstrations of Nondirective Teaching and analyze your peer teaching and that of others. It will also be used for microteaching (teaching small groups of children) and for general classroom observation.

The Guide emphasizes what we consider to be the essential features of the Nondirective stance. With some models of teaching, the Guide can specify particular teaching skills and definitive phases of the model. In Nondirective Teaching, however, the learner participates so fully in the determination of events that no prescribed sequence can be made, and the counseling interview can turn out in a variety of ways. Thus, this guide is designed to help you look for particular dimensions of Nondirective Teaching and to determine if the person being observed—whether yourself or someone else—is dealing with those dimensions.

The Problematic Dimension

In most school situations, Nondirective Teaching occurs because there is a problem that is perceived by the student or the teacher. Unless the problem—or at least the student's feelings about the problem—is explored, Nondirective Teaching can wander in circles. In the space below, indicate your observations about the teacher's ability to help the student define the problem in cognitive and affective terms and reflect to himself where he stands in the problem area. Then, in the rating form to the right, judge the adequacy with which the teacher fulfilled this dimension of Nondirective Teaching.

Thoroughly	Partially	Missing	Not Needed

Maintaining an Equal Role

One of the essential features of Nondirective Teaching is maintaining an egalitarian relationship with the student. In the interview, the teacher is definitely the teacher, just as a counselor is definitely a counselor, but this role implies *function* rather than *status*. If the teacher gives greater weight to his or her own ideas than to the student's ideas, the relationship that is essential for nondirection is destroyed. The teacher may provide ideas or wisdom, but is not to be superior. In the space below, jot down your general assessment of the teacher's ability to maintain an egalitarian stance. Then provide a rating.

Thoroughly	Partially	Missing	Not Needed

155

TEACHING ANALYSIS GUIDE FOR NONDIRECTIVE TEACHING

The Nondirective Dimension

Did the teacher maintain a relatively nondirective stance? That is, did the teacher seek the frame of reference of the student and help the student to understand himself in relation to the problem under consideration? This stance contrasts sharply with an instructive stance, where the teacher seeks an opportunity to provide information or ideas external to the student's frame of reference. Nondirection means exactly that. The teacher is not there to direct, but to facilitate. The teacher may take the lead at times, but primarily to help the student understand himself and come to grips with his own problems rather than to provide information or concepts that are unrelated to the student's self-concept and perception of his world. Comment below on the success of the teacher in upholding the nondirective dimension, and then supply a rating.

Thoroughly	Partially	Missing	Not Needed

Expression of Feelings

The expression of feelings (often referred to as catharsis) enables the learner to vent his emotions and begin to come to grips with himself as an emotional as well as a cognitive being. Without the expression of feelings, Nondirective Teaching is dry and empty. In the space below, put down your observations about the ability of the teacher to elicit feelings from the learner, to accept them, and to encourage their expression while helping the student understand them. Then provide a rating.

Thoroughly	Partially	Missing	Not Needed

The Skills Dimensions

Reflecting, probing, and lead taking are among the specific skills that aid the facilitative process of Nondirective Teaching. Various skills are needed at various times. Indicate in the space below the kinds of skills that the teacher used and your view of the extent to which the teacher was able to use them appropriately and strongly. In the rating form to the right, indicate the adequacy with which you feel the teacher displayed the skills called for by the nondirective stance.

Thoroughly	Partially	Missing	Not Needed

TEACHING ANALYSIS GUIDE FOR NONDIRECTIVE TEACHING

Next Steps

Nondirective interviews often seem somewhat inconclusive in contrast with instructional encounters. Nonetheless, the student comes to the nondirective interview to learn, as much as he comes to directive instruction to learn. One of the most important dimensions in a successful interview is the establishment of a common frame of reference between teacher and learner that leads to future interviews or helps the individual develop a way of approaching his future. What we are concerned with here is the establishment, at some point, of a reasonable focus for the learner. He should become aware of his feelings, or of a better definition of the problem, or of something he is going to work on before the next interview. In the space below, comment on how successfully a common frame of reference was established that would lead to follow-up steps. Judge the adequacy with which a theme was established that could provide continuity as the learner struggles with his problems.

Thoroughly	Partially	Missing	Not Needed

AFTER PEER TEACHING: MICROTEACHING

Peer teaching was an opportunity to "walk through" the pattern of the Nondirective Interview strategy. The Teaching Analysis Guide should have helped you identify areas of your understanding or performance that need further development. Aside from the specifics of the Teaching Analysis Guide, we would like you to reflect intuitively on your peer teaching experience. Did you feel that you were able to maintain the nondirective strategy? Were you able to give up the traditional teacher role and assume the role of counselor or facilitator?

As you prepare for microteaching, identify aspects of the nondirective strategy that you would like to improve upon. Usually, this means assuming more of a listening role, concentrating more on the student's responses, becoming more flexible in your responses to the student's feelings, and becoming more selective in nondirective lead-taking moves. We suggest that you mentally "walk through" another nondirective interview before you microteach.

If you worked with a peer in using the Nondirective Interview strategy, you may want to try the strategy now with a student. Again, record your interview on tape and analyze it with the Teaching Analysis Guide. This will allow you to concentrate on the Nondirective Interview strategy and not be concerned with remembering what you did when you fill in the Guide later.

At this point you have a choice: you may microteach with a single student, or you may try the nondirective strategy with several students in a small group activity. In either case, it will be natural for you to wonder, "Am I doing this right?" Except for glaring omissions or commissions that may have emerged in your peer teaching, the refinement of the model depends on your willingness to listen and respond to the student, to accept his or her point of view. The Nondirective Model will seem more natural if you are able to relax and concentrate on the student and not on your own responses. If you have internalized the basic *goals*,

157

principles, and procedures of the model, now is the time to shift from an external way of thinking to an internal one.

We suggest audio-taping the microteaching so that you can reflect on the lesson afterwards. Student(s) will respond differently from your peer or student in the peer teaching session. It is a good idea to use the Teaching Analysis Guide with the microteaching lesson. You may also want to share the experience with your colleagues and receive their comments and suggestions.

The fourth and last component of the Nondirective Model suggests how to adapt the model to an entire class and how to incorporate other models with Nondirective Teaching. The emphasis of your training in this model will gradually shift now from mastering the basic elements to designing and applying the model in the classroom.

Component IV

ADAPTING
THE MODEL

AN OPEN ENVIRONMENT APPROACH
BASED ON NONDIRECTIVE PRINCIPLES

The Nondirective Model is appropriate for individual (the interview), group discussion, or classroom environment use. A classroom that uses the model is commonly called an open classroom and has the following characteristics: First, its *objectives* are affective development, growth of student self-concept, and student determination of learning needs. Second, its *methods* of instruction are directed toward student flexibility in learning. Group work that concentrates on creativity and self-knowledge is the main instructional technique. Third, the *teacher's role* is that of a facilitator, resource person, guide, and advisor. Fourth, *the student determines what is important* to learn. He is free to set his own educational objectives and to select the method(s) for attaining his goals. Fifth, the *evaluation* of progress in the classroom consists more of student self-evaluation than of teacher evaluation. Progress is measured qualitatively rather than quantitatively.

The goals of the Nondirective Model in the classroom are to help students take responsibility for their own learning and to provide a framework in which students can learn with as much or as little help as they need. Knowledge based only on facts can become obsolete faster than we can learn it. The Nondirective model asks: Why not teach students the skills for learning rather than a series of facts, which constantly change as new knowledge is added? We need to teach specific facts only when we desire to use them as a way of preserving part of our culture. Thus, we will never escape the need to teach that July 4, 1776 was the date of the Declaration of Independence, but the meaning of this document can be taught in fashions other than the memorizing of facts. Similarly, we can teach about works of literature, but the students can never experience the meaning of the writing until they have read the works with real interest.

Drawing on the two assumptions that students should take responsibility for their own learning and that students should be provided with help as they need it, we shall discuss in this component the use of the Nondirective Teaching Model in the classroom.

One of the important uses of Nondirective Teaching occurs when a class becomes stale and the teacher finds herself pushing or pulling the students through exercises and subject matter. One sixth-grade teacher, exhausted by the failure of more traditional attempts to cope with the discipline problems and the lack of interest in her class, decided to experiment with student-centered teaching. She turned to Nondirective approaches in order to help her students take more responsibility for their learning and to ensure that the subject matter would be related to their needs and learning styles. She has provided an account of that experience, from which excerpts are presented here:

March 5, We Begin

A week ago I decided to initiate a new program in my sixth grade classroom, based on student-centered teaching—an unstructured or non-directive approach.

I began by telling the class that we were going to try an "experiment." I explained that for one day I would let them do anything they wanted to do—they did not have to do anything if they did not want to.

Many started with art projects; some drew or painted most of the day. Others read or did work in math and other subjects. There was an air of excitement all day. Many were so interested in what they were doing that they did not want to go out at recess or noon!

At the end of the day I asked the class to evaluate the experiment. The comments were most interesting. Some were "confused," distressed without the teacher telling them what to do, without specific assignments to complete.

The majority of the class thought the day was "great," but some expressed concern over the noise level and the fact that a few "goofed off" all day. Most felt that they had accomplished as much work as we usually do, and they enjoyed being able to work at a task until it was completed, without the pressure of a time limit. They liked doing things without being "forced" to do them and liked deciding what to do.

They begged to continue the "experiment" so it was decided to do so, for two more days. We would then re-evaluate the plan.

The next morning I implemented the idea of a "work contract." I gave them ditto sheets listing all our subjects with suggestions under each. There was a space provided for their "plans" in each area and for checking upon completion.

Each child was to write his or her contract for the day—choosing the areas in which he would work and planning specifically what he would do. Upon completion of any exercise, drill, review, etc., he was to check and correct his own work, using the teacher's manual. The work was to be kept in a folder with the contract.

I met with each child to discuss his plans. Some completed theirs in a very short time; we discussed as a group what this might mean, and what to do about it. It was suggested that the plan might not be challenging enough, that an adjustment should be made—perhaps going on or adding another area to the day's plan.

Resource materials were provided, suggestions made, and drill materials made available to use when needed.

I found I had much more time, so I worked, talked, and spent the time with individuals and groups. At the end of the third day I evaluated the work folder with each child. To solve the problem of grades, I had each child tell me what he thought he had earned.

March 12, Progress Report

Our "experiment" has, in fact, become our program—with some adjustments.

Some children continued to be frustrated and felt insecure without teacher direction. Discipline also continued to be a problem with some, and I began to realize that, although the children involved may need the program more than the others, I was expecting too much from them, too soon—they were not ready to assume self-direction yet. Perhaps a gradual weaning from the spoon-fed procedures was necessary.

I regrouped the class—creating two groups. The largest group is the non-directed. The smallest is teacher-directed, made up of children who wanted to return to the former teacher-directed method, and those who, for varied reasons were unable to function in the self-directed situation.

I would have waited longer to see what would have happened, but the situation for some disintegrated a little more each day—penalizing the whole class. The disrupting factor kept everyone upset and limited those who wanted to study and work. So it seemed to me best for the group as a whole as well as the program to modify the plan.

Those who continued the "experiment" have forged ahead. I showed them how to program their work, using their texts as a basic guide. They have learned that they can teach themselves (and each other) and that I am available when a step is not clear or advice is needed.

At the end of the week they evaluate themselves in each area—in terms of work accomplished, accuracy, etc. We have learned that the number of errors is not a criterion of failure or success. Errors can and should be part of the learning process; we learn through our mistakes. We also discussed the fact that consistently perfect scores may mean that the work is not challenging enough and perhaps we should move on.

After self-evaluation, each child brings the evaluation sheet and work folder to discuss with me.

Some of the members of the group working with me are most anxious to become "independent" students. We will evaluate together each week their progress toward that goal.

I have only experienced one parental objection so far. A parent felt her child was not able to function without direction.

Some students (there were two or three) who originally wanted to return to the teacher-directed program are now anticipating going back into the self-directed program. (I sense that it has been difficult for them to readjust to the old program as it would be for me to do so.)[1]

As you can tell from this account, the Nondirective Model is not easy for the teacher. The Nondirective teacher does not simply turn over the room to the students and withdraw from the activity; rather, he or she maintains an integral role in the classroom. Nondirective teaching is not an abrogation of responsibility but a shifting of decision making in the classroom. Decisions are no longer made solely by the teacher; they are made in conjunction with the students, because the students have set the goals for the learning. For some students, unable to cope with the decisions that are necessary in this model, the teacher will have to make some of the decisions. But the judgment that these decisions will have to be made by the teacher is made in conjunction with the student.

In the Nondirective classroom, the teacher functions as a facilitator, helping students learn what is important to them. The successful facilitator has a number of qualities that Carl Rogers has identified as appropriate for the successful group leader or counselor. But the role is different when the facilitator is a teacher. First, the teacher must be a real person who accepts each student as an individual and is able to separate himself as a teacher from the work that is being assigned. The realness of the teacher is important in all areas of personal relationship with the student. The teacher can respond as he feels and can accept honest responses from the students. The teacher must be able to separate the students' work from the students themselves. A poorly done assignment does not mean the student is a poorly made student.

Willingness to accept and to trust students is the second quality valued in the teacher in the facilitating role. This characteristic helps a teacher to develop realness. The teacher cares that the student learns, but the teacher is not possessive. The student is accepted as an individual who is worthy of trust. Basic to the Nondirective Model is the idea that students are trustworthy when given responsibility. The trust between student and teacher forms a personal contract that binds them to work together. But students are students, and often the contract is broken. Sometimes this is done unintentionally, but if the students come to realize that the contract is not a good one or that they are not ready for the commitment, it can be done deliberately. This is the point at which the most trust is necessary. The teacher must be willing to trust the students and begin again. Or he must agree with the students on how to rewrite the contract with new goals, and perhaps more control by the teacher.

The third characteristic of a teacher who is a successful facilitator is empathy, the ability to look at a situation as the student or students see it. Empathetic understanding is not saying, "I know what is wrong with you." It is understanding that is nonevaluative; it is viewing the situation as the students see it with sympathy for their point of view. Realizing the many difficulties that can occur when a teacher tries to become a facilitator, Rogers notes,

When a facilitator creates, even to a modest degree, a classroom climate characterized by all that he can achieve of realness, prizing, and empathy;

---

[1] Carl R. Rogers, *Freedom to Learn* (Columbus, Ohio: Charles E. Merrill, 1969), pp. 12-16. Reprinted by permission of Charles E. Merrill.

when he trusts the constructive tendency of the individual and the group; then he discovers that he has inaugurated an educational revolution. Learning of a different quality, proceeding at a different pace, with a greater degree of pervasiveness, occurs. Feelings—positive, negative, confused—become part of the classroom experience. Learning becomes life, and a very vital part at that. The student is on his way, sometimes excitedly, sometimes reluctantly, to become a learning, changing being.[2]

How can the facilitator create the classroom environment characterized by realness, prizing, and empathy? Teachers begin by dealing with the problems as the students see them. In a classroom, this may mean that students work on more than one project simultaneously. Sometimes it may mean being honest and saying that the course is a requirement, and that if the students seem to have no interest, the teacher must present possible topics. In the case of students without a learning interest, the teacher may need to draw on other teaching skills to help the students find issues or areas in the subject that they are interested in. Models such as Simulation and Inquiry Training will be helpful in these situations. But most students have concerns and interests that, if tapped, can lead them to become students with whom it is easy to establish a relationship that is real, prizing, and empathetic.

How does the teacher function in the Nondirective role? According to Rogers,

> When a teacher is concerned with the facilitation of learning rather than the function of teaching, he organizes his time very differently from the conventional teacher. Instead of spending great blocs of time organizing lesson plans and lectures, he concentrates on providing all kinds of resources which will give his students experiential learning relevant to their needs. He also concentrates on making such resources clearly available, by thinking through and simplifying the practical and psychological steps which the student must go through in order to utilize the resources.[3]

Rogers elaborates by saying that it is one thing to suggest books to read, and another to collect books and other resources and bring them into the classroom so that they are easily available for students to explore and use. By resources, Rogers means books, articles, work space, a laboratory room, equipment, tools, maps, films, and recordings, as well as human resources.

In addition to providing resources for the students, the teacher can use contracts to facilitate the learning. About contracts, Rogers says,

> One open-ended device which helps to give both security and responsibility within an atmosphere of freedom is the use of student contracts. There is no doubt that this also helps assuage the uncertainties and insecurities which the facilitator may be experiencing. . . . This enables the pupil to set a goal for himself and to plan what he wishes to do. It provides a sort of transitional experience between complete freedom to learn whatever is of interest, and learning which is relatively free but which is within the limits of some institutional demand.[4]

[2] *Ibid.*, p. 115.
[3] *Ibid.*, p. 131.
[4] *Ibid.*, p. 133.

A third resource for student learning is the use of programmed instruction. The use of shorter programs that teach specific content or skills can be very efficient for both learner and teacher. The student is able to progress at his own rate and to select the material that will interest him the most. Programmed instruction can also provide the necessary structure for students who seem, at first, to be unable to cope with the freedom available in the nondirective classroom.

The most basic way to implement the Rogerian model in the classroom environment is through the use of groups. Groups can be formed on the basis of student interests, and they can become self-governing bodies whose members work together to solve problems or explore interests. It would be naive to assume that a teacher can simply say to a group, "Form," and the group will form and function easily. This is not the case. The teacher must help the groups establish themselves and must provide some structure so that there is a procedure to be followed. Guidelines supplied by the teacher are not necessarily a violation of the basic premises of the Rogerian classroom model. In fact, they form a basis upon which the Nondirective Model can function easily in the classroom. Some of the items that a teacher may choose to control are the size of the group, how often the group must report on its progress, procedures for asking for teacher help, and guidelines for class members about how to participate in a group.

The final responsibility of the nondirective teacher is to establish mechanisms for self-evaluation. This is crucial if the students are to be allowed to direct and initiate the focus of their own learning. It is essential that the students be involved in all stages of the evaluation of their learning. Through student self-evaluation, the teacher is able to help the students judge how well they are functioning as group members and whether or not they are learning what they want to achieve. The most efficient way to handle this situation is a conference between student and teacher. Each appraises the progress that has been made, and the two negotiate the conclusion of the evaluation in an appropriate manner—a grade or a progress report. The nondirective interview is an appropriate technique for helping students evaluate their work.

The decision to use the nondirective strategy with an entire class is not an easy decision for most teachers. But once made, the decision alters significantly the perceptions of students and their part in classroom learning. Skillful adaptation of the nondirective interview strategy can provide a base for negotiations with the students concerning a sharing of responsibility for their own learning. The close parallels between the individual and classroom use of the model can be seen in Figure 1.

COMBINING THE NONDIRECTIVE MODEL WITH OTHER MODELS OF TEACHING

Using an open-environment approach to learning, Nondirective Teaching can incorporate all of the other learning models. The Information Processing Models can be used to help students explore facts, problems, and ideas they want to learn more about. Inquiry Training can be used to stimulate student interest in required subjects, and Concept Attainment can help students deal with ideas that are intriguing, new, and complex. The Advance Organizer's stress on verbal learning can

Phase One	Phase Two	Phase Three

Teacher establishes an accepting climate
    trust
    prizing
    empathy
	Encouragement
	    individual expression
	    from teacher and
	    students
	    clarification of
	    accepting climate
		Groups and individuals identify and pursue learning goals.

Phase Four	Phase Five

Self-evaluation
    Teacher is trusting, prizing, has empathy.
    Decisions are made together.
	Integration
	    identification of a second series of problems
	    cycle begins again

Figure 1. *Phases of the Rogerian Classroom Model.*

be conveyed to students through tutorials, programmed instruction, and differentiated roles within groups, depending on the students' interest in and knowledge of the subject matter.

In the social family, the Jurisprudential Model can help students analyze issues of interest and complexity. Through Role Playing and Simulation, the students' attention can be directed or attracted to problems that are new, confusing, and challenging to their values. Synectics can be used to spark creativity in an individual or a group, or through programmed instructional material.

The Nondirective Model is a total approach to the classroom. It may be used effectively with a single individual, as a technique for group work, or for an entire classroom. If it is used with the whole class, all of the other models of teaching complement it and are effective in promoting student-directed learning.

INDEX